Praise for *Angel Dogs with a Mission*

"Allen and Linda Anderson have gathered charming tales of canine love and loyalty that will remind readers why Fido's name means faith."

— Gary Kowalski, author of *The Souls of Animals* and *Goodbye, Friend*

"*Angel Dogs with a Mission* is a celebration of the intelligence, courage, and compassion of the remarkable canine souls with whom we have the honor of sharing this planet and our lives. In this gorgeous collection of brilliant stories, the dogs' actions speak for themselves, proving that they have a masterful sense of intelligence and an undeniable ability to reason. But their amazing intelligence is only overshadowed by the size of their hearts."

— Amelia Kinkade, author of *Straight from the Horse's Mouth: How to Talk to Animals and Get Answers* and *The Language of Miracles*

Praise for *Angel Dogs*

"Reading *Angel Dogs: Divine Messengers of Comfort* is like taking a walk in the park on a sunny day with your favorite dog. This wonderful collection of stories will bring back memories of the sweet, delightful, and touching times you have spent with your own loyal canine friends."

— from the foreword by Willard Scott, NBC's *Today* show

"The Andersons have done it again! *Angel Dogs* is a healing and heart-opening book. Highly recommended."

— Doreen Virtue, PhD, author of *Angel Medicine* and *Healing with the Angels*

Praise for *Angel Cats*

"Angels come to us in many ways. Some are never identified, some come to us and we don't even know they changed our lives, maybe even saved us, until there is a realization. This book is enlightening and will make you take many a close look at your 'angel.'"

— Tippi Hedren, actress and animal activist

"As a believer and one who lives the message, my heart was touched by *Angel Cats*. I have long realized that it is not an accident that three-quarters of our lifeline is feline. So read, laugh, cry, and become a more complete human being through the angel cats and the lifeline they provide."

— Bernie Siegel, MD, author of *365 Prescriptions for the Soul* and *Love, Medicine & Miracles*

Praise for *Rescued: Saving Animals from Disaster*

"Compelling, fascinating, and, most important, highly moral."

— Ben Stein, author, actor, and commentator

"A must-read that I couldn't put down, *Rescued* will move you to action."

— Marc Bekoff, professor emeritus of biology at the University of Colorado and editor of the *Encyclopedia of Animal Behavior*

"*Rescued* serves as a reminder that saving animals' precious lives is not only noble but also a moral imperative."

— Gretchen Wyler, vice president of the Humane Society of the United States (Hollywood Office) and retired executive producer of the Genesis Awards

"The book offers vital, in-the-trenches information for saving animals' lives.... Read it and reap!"

— Marty Becker, DVM, resident veterinarian on *Good Morning America* and the author of *The Healing Power of Pets*

ANGEL DOGS
with a MISSION

Joy,

A very Merry Christmas (?)
And a Happy New Year.

With belated love and
very best wishes for 2010.

John + Joey
(x)   xxxx

Christmas 2009

Also by Allen and Linda Anderson

Angel Animals: Divine Messengers of Miracles

Angel Cats: Divine Messengers of Comfort

Angel Dogs: Divine Messengers of Love

Angel Horses: Divine Messengers of Hope

God's Messengers: What Animals Teach Us about the Divine

Rainbows and Bridges: An Animal Companion Memorial Kit

Rescued: Saving Animals from Disaster

Saying Goodbye to Your Angel Animals:
Finding Comfort after Losing Your Pet

ANGEL DOGS
with a MISSION

Divine Messengers
in Service to All Life

Allen & Linda Anderson
Foreword by Marc Bekoff

New World Library
Novato, California

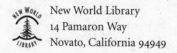

New World Library
14 Pamaron Way
Novato, California 94949

Text design by Tona Pearce Myers

Library of Congress Cataloging-in-Publication Data
Angel dogs with a mission : divine messengers in service to all life / [edited by]
   Allen and Linda Anderson ; foreword by Marc Bekoff.
      p.   cm.
Includes bibliographical references.
ISBN 978-1-57731-602-2 (pbk. : alk. paper)
1. Dogs—United States—Anecdotes. 2. Dog owners—United States—Anecdotes.
3. Human-animal relationships—United States—Anecdotes. I. Anderson, Allen.
II. Anderson, Linda C.
SF426.2.A527 2008
636.7—dc22   2008024974

First printing, September 2008
ISBN 978-1-57731-602-2
Printed in Canada on 100% postconsumer-waste recycled paper

 New World Library is a proud member of the Green Press Initiative.

10   9   8   7   6   5   4   3   2   1

To Prana, Taylor, and Leaf, our angel dogs with a mission

Contents

Chapter Four: A Mission to Protect

Chapter Five: A Mission to Teach

Chapter Six: A Mission to Bring Joy and Hope

Dogs Are the Way to Increase Our Compassionate Footprint

*I*f anyone doubts that dogs respond to humans with compassion and empathy, this book will sweep away those uncertainties. It will surely force the few skeptics out there to reconsider how far the canine-human relationship has evolved and how deep it can be. *Angel Dogs with a Mission* demonstrates, in story after story, that dogs have distinct personalities, are able to solve complex problems, and have the cognitive and emotional capacities to assess a current situation, do what's right, and plan for the future. This heartwarming book considers not only *how* dogs perform their exemplary and courageous acts of service but also *why* they choose to give of themselves with such selflessness. They don't have to do what they do. They aren't coerced to show loyalty and love.

Considerable scientific data show that animals have a therapeutic effect on the humans who bring them into their homes or welcome them into their lives in other venues, including hospitals, assisted-living facilities, and jails. Lower blood pressure, decreased stress, and the alleviation of loneliness are some of the many benefits of bonding with an animal. Dog companions offer the additional perk of needing to be walked, which requires their human companions to make physical exercise part of their daily routines. But what is it in a dog's emotional makeup that inspires people to rise above the circumstances of their lives and do things they could never have imagined?

Allen and Linda Anderson have interviewed people whose lives were changed for the better by a dog. The Andersons explore the spiritual qualities that dogs demonstrate, an area that is largely uncharted in today's world. This collection of stories takes us on a journey into the dog's deep capacity for compassion and empathy. Going beyond pure instinct, training, and individual personalities, these stories portray dogs interacting with people and other animals by choosing to be there for them. By observing, accompanying, and being recipients of the dog's sensitivity, skill, and courage, these contributors, and indeed all of us, are inspired to become better human beings. Close relationships with dogs and other animals are a wonderful means for increasing our compassionate footprint. It's a win-win situation for all. Compassion readily spreads across species, and there's no better way to make the world a better home for all beings, a place where we can all peacefully coexist on a planet that is typically dominated by humans.

Because I'm on the faculty of Bonnie Bergin's Assistance Dog

Institute, I was especially drawn to Bonnie's and Kerry Knaus-Hardy's experiences with a mixed-breed dog named Abdul. Both Bonnie and Kerry acknowledge that without Abdul, the idea of teaching dogs to serve people with physical disabilities would not have become reality in the way and at the time that it did. During the mid-1970s the concept of a dog coming to the aid of a wheelchair-bound person with severe physical disabilities was unheard of and untried. Abdul's unique personality, love, and ability to communicate with Kerry showed what is possible. This wonderful dog became a beacon of hope around the world for the training of other service dogs.

Over and over again, the stories in this book show that a willing and determined dog can transform the impossible into the possible. They tell of dogs who saved people's lives and who acted as catalysts for the betterment of their fellow animals and of humans. From Sarah Atlas's dog Anna serving at Ground Zero on September 11 to Lisa LaVerdier's Home for Life rescued dogs providing purpose to at-risk teenage boys, from Dr. Karla Rose's Tuffy giving comfort to students and staff after the Virginia Tech tragedy to Deb Richeson's Welsh Corgi listening as children read and thereby raising school test scores, this book contains behind-the-scenes stories of dogs who made news headlines. But beyond anything that the media covered, the Andersons have asked the kinds of questions that caused contributors to reveal never-before-told information about how their lives have been touched and changed by a dog.

As a card-carrying scientist, an ethologist and behavioral ecologist who specializes in drawing attention to the rich emotional lives of animals, for decades I have observed and closely studied the empathy that dogs regularly and openly display. This book blurs —

truly dismantles — the supposed line between the feelings that humans experience and those present in animals. It reveals individual dogs' unique personalities and sheds light on the complexities of animal behavior. *Angel Dogs with a Mission* provides first-hand accounts, rich in texture and imagery, to broaden and deepen our collective awareness of the minds, the hearts, and as the Andersons would say, the loving souls of dogs. Read this book and share it widely. Read these stories to kids. *Angel Dogs with a Mission* will change your life and the lives of those with whom you share it.

— Marc Bekoff, author of
The Emotional Lives of Animals, Animals Matter, Animals at Play: Rules of the Game, and *Wild Justice: Reflections on Empathy, Fair Play, and Morality in Animals* and editor of *The Encyclopedia of Human-Animal Relationships* (http://literati.net/Bekoff)

Service to All Life

But I have promises to keep...

— Robert Frost

This is going to sound like a strange introduction, but it's absolutely true. Because we took time out to write this book for you, our friends, co-workers, and family members were spared momentarily. *You* will now be the recipients of our enthusiasm for the dogs and humans who inspired us to rave about them to everyone who would listen.

It's not that those close to us are indifferent to our passion for animals. Since 1996, when we founded the Angel Animals Network, friends and family have cheered us on and lifted us through the tough times. When we dropped off the face of the planet while researching, writing, and promoting our books, they were patient, supportive, and generous.

But while we were writing *Angel Dogs with a Mission*, people who knew us started to hesitate before asking, "What's new?" They knew that we would deluge them with little-known facts and jaw-dropping stories about dogs and people who had impressed us. After interviewing the contributing authors and gathering these stories, we marveled at the dogs' range of talents and experiences. Their abilities went far beyond the expectations of scientists or animal-behavior experts.

More about Purpose

Some of the dogs in this book are celebrities who have appeared on television talk shows, are the stars of reenactments, or were subjects of newspaper and magazine articles. Although a few story contributors had previously talked to the media, they revealed new information to us. This is because we asked questions that evoked deeper reflection about the spiritual significance of their dogs' purpose in life.

Missions, callings, vocations, and purposes are words usually associated with humans, yet dogs seek to have more meaning in their lives too. They give selflessly and never look back with regret for what might have been. Dogs find and fulfill the promise of all they were meant to be.

Regardless of training and breeding, the dogs in this anthology show canines making sensitive, conscious, and compassionate choices as they serve, protect, heal, amuse, teach, and inspire. These dogs plan strategies, extrapolate from the known to the unknown, are creative and intuitive, show incredible focus and persistence, and act ethically. They love and serve without expecting a return. Nonetheless, treats and rewards are always welcome.

The dogs in this book make it clear that they want more out of life than lounging around and soaking up the sun. They refuse to succumb to malaise and wantonness.

Typically these dogs are family pets who needed a job to occupy their amazing minds and abilities. Some — like livestock dogs, dog guides for the blind, military or law enforcement dogs, and service dogs for people with physical disabilities — are specifically bred or trained for their work. In other cases, the dogs took it upon themselves, with no human enticement or request, to offer assistance to other dogs and people in need. Yet when the day's tasks are finished, even the most carefully trained and disciplined dogs turned into playful companions and pets.

We were impressed by the ways dogs showed they looked forward to working and giving service. Many dogs prepared with special training courses and certifications. They usually dressed for success, changing from a fun-loving pal into a working partner upon donning a service vest, kerchief, or whatever indicated to them that it was time to report for duty. Repeatedly the storytellers told us how amazing it was to watch a relaxed, even somewhat goofy, dog put on a uniform and transform into a focused, eager worker.

Every dog book lauds dogs for their loyalty, courage, and unconditional love. The dogs we met through these stories demonstrate those qualities not only for their human family members but also for strangers in need. They found the lost and comforted the grieving.

We noticed that dogs who should be filled with rage and bitterness at humans for abusing, neglecting, and abandoning them learned to trust again. Yet they went far beyond forgiveness. They served unstintingly and rescued heroically.

Sacred Agreements

Writing this book made us think more deeply about the concept of sacred agreements. When dogs and humans spiritually connect with each other, they bear witness to the idea that some encounters are just meant to be. Call it destiny, fate, karma, or divine intervention, people and animals meet, teach, and learn from each other in the most miraculous and unexpected ways.

Some religious traditions hold the belief that prior to entering a lifetime, souls agree to meet and help each other take their next spiritual steps. As the journeys chronicled here unfolded, it was breathtaking to us how perfectly timed the entrances and exits of dogs and people turned out to be. If A had not occurred, B and C would not have been possible. Humans and dogs kept their sacred agreements with remarkable precision. From the centers of these spiritual relationships, mutual love and respect rippled into the world and nourished all life.

The Dogs You'll Meet

It is our pleasure and honor to introduce you to some of the most incredible dogs on the planet. You'll meet dogs who have saved people's and animals' lives, given hope to troubled teenagers, brought joy and consolation to people who were injured, and became indispensable partners and fellow teachers.

The following are previews from some of the twenty dramatic true stories that amazed and delighted us:

For two years, Robin Siggers, a member of the Canadian Avalanche Rescue Dog Association, arduously trained his Lab-collie–mix puppy, Keno, to be an avalanche search dog. All their rehearsal paid off when a ski resort employee became buried in an avalanche with no way for patrollers to locate him and the inability to survive more than thirty minutes.

Bonnie Bergin, founder of Canine Companions for Independence and the Assistance Dog Institute, trained a rambunctious puppy named Abdul to be the first service dog for a person with disabilities. The account of Bonnie's pioneering concept is followed by the never-before-published story of Kerrill Knaus-Hardy, the first person with physical disabilities, other than deafness and blindness, to work with and adopt a trained service dog.

Midge, a Chihuahua–rat terrier mix, has the distinction of being the Guinness World Record holder as the smallest police dog. She encourages Ohio schoolchildren never to let tiny size stop them from following their dreams.

Marvin, a lame Rhode Island SPCA animal-shelter dog turned family pet, paints and exhibits his artwork and visits schools and nursing homes. This nonprofit animal shelter uses the sale of MarvArt to provide medical services that help elderly and sick people to keep their pets.

Sarah Atlas's dog, Anna, died shortly after serving as one of the first dogs to conduct searches and offer comfort at Ground Zero after the tragic events of September 11, 2001. Anna inspired Sarah to start an assistance program for handlers of search-and-rescue dogs.

Di Thompson shares her wonderful story about Angel, a bedraggled and abused puppy who instinctively knew which people and animals needed her healing presence. Di and Angel's story was the winner of the 2007 contest we sponsored to find stories for this book.

Tuffy, a canine therapy dog, worked side by side with Boston's Dr. Karla Rose, a skilled grief and trauma counselor, as the team helped to heal students, staff, and personnel at the Virginia Tech campus after a rampage that resulted in the deaths of thirty-two faculty members and students.

Kobi, a beloved family pet with an exceptional sense of smell and intelligence, became one of the most famous cancer-sniffing dogs in the world and contributed to the Pine Street Foundation's breakthrough research for combating this deadly disease.

Lt. Col. Christopher P. Coppola, USAF, shares his experiences with German shepherds trained to be military dogs, who show courage and loyalty as they protect and save the lives of their handlers and other soldiers in Iraq. The dogs bring the comforts of companionship to a war-zone hospital.

Zoom, a little Welsh corgi with a big heart, made national news when he helped to raise reading test scores in a rural Kentucky school. He serves as the children's rapt listener while they read to him and offers canine stress relief to the school's teachers.

Kutty and Goldie, brought into service by Mrs. Minal Vishal Kavishwar, are India's first dogs trained according to international standards and certified as therapy dogs by the Delta Society. A nonprofit organization, the Delta Society's mission is to expand and support the role of service and therapy animals for the improvement of human health and education. Mrs. Kavishwar won the Delta Society's 2007 Beyond Limits award for bringing her therapy dog teams to special schools for the mentally challenged. She was honored for creating an effective clinical psychology practice that overcame geographical and cultural challenges.

Skidboot, the world-famous Texas blue heeler of cowboy David Hartwig, appeared on *The Tonight Show with Jay Leno*, *The Oprah Winfrey Show*, *Late Show with David Letterman*, and other shows, bringing joy to millions with his amazing intelligence and unflappable gentility.

Allen's personal story shares the miracles he experienced after rescuing our cocker spaniel, Leaf. This story poses a question we often hear: who does most of the rescuing when you adopt an animal in need, you or the dog?

In the back of this book we have included biographical information about the contributing authors. In a world where bad news and misdeeds often dominate, it's uplifting to know how much good one person and one dog can do.

We have written brief meditations for you to use, if you wish, as a guide for contemplating how to apply the wisdom in these stories for fulfilling your own life's purpose.

Join us now in venturing to places on earth and in the heavens that only seem accessible if you follow a canine's lead.

CHAPTER ONE

A Mission to Serve

Celebrate your purpose and be grateful for it. It is a gift; indeed, it is a double gift, one that you bestow to others and one that has been bestowed on you. You are fortunate to have a noble purpose, and the rest of the world is fortunate that you have one.

— William Damon

Keno, the Wonder Dog, Delivers an Avalanche Miracle

Robin Siggers
Fernie, British Columbia, Canada

S ince 1979 I've been a ski patroller and avalanche forecaster working in a winter paradise. The Rocky Mountains of British Columbia offer one of the world's most pristine and adventurous areas for outdoor sports. As peaceful as the snow-capped mountains appear to be, they are also fraught with danger. Deep snow and steep slopes combine to pose the constant risk of avalanche. Skiers and boarders must always be on their guard.

With as many as sixteen people killed each year in avalanches in Canada, highly efficient handler-and-dog search teams are essential for mountain safety. An avalanche travels from sixty to a hundred miles per hour, and the victim has only a 50 percent chance of surviving more than twenty-five minutes. Ninety-five percent of avalanche victims die within the first two hours.[1]

In the mid-eighties I met Sue Boyd, another ski patroller who had an avalanche search dog. Watching Sue and her dog together made me consider dog handling as a way to expand my horizons. I got a dog and started training with the Canadian Avalanche Rescue Dog Association (CARDA), a nonprofit charitable organization that provides excellent avalanche search-and-rescue team training for Canada.

The CARDA website says that avalanche dogs can do a coarse search of an area in thirty minutes, whereas humans using probes would take up to four hours searching the same area.[2] With a dog's heightened olfactory ability, the animal can pick up the scent of a person below as much as twelve feet of snow. Although weather conditions affect the outcome of an accident, time becomes the major factor in whether someone will live or die after being buried under mounds of snow and ice.

Keno, the Survivor

In 1996 my first dog, K2, was getting on in years. To further my avalanche rescue interest, I adopted a new puppy named Keno, the only survivor of a litter. Keno's mother was Sue's purebred chocolate Labrador retriever, a trained avalanche rescue dog. The neighbor's dog, a collie named Lucky, had jumped the fence and bred with Keno's mother. This made Keno a rare, strangely beautiful golden Lab, whose thick coat of alabaster fur gave the impression that dog and snow were one. Despite the freezing-cold weather in the Rocky Mountains of British Columbia, Keno's wagging tail and friendly disposition warmed the hearts of everyone who met him.

Keno was a pleasant, sociable dog, but he did not like being petted on the head. If someone came near, he would sniff and be friendly but back away from letting the person pet anything other than his rump. It was as if he sensed he had an important job to do that commanded more respect than most people show to an ordinary dog with a pat on the head.

Keno was a puppy when I first met him, and I observed that he was big, fat, and healthy. His hardy body made me think he would be well suited for outdoor search-and-rescue work in the mountains. Keno enjoyed rolling around in the snow. If he found even a patch, he'd tumble in it. Later, I reflected on how surprisingly appropriate it was that this dog who had been the only survivor of his litter, had a father named Lucky, and loved snow became one of the world's best-known avalanche search-and-rescue dogs.

Keno's Training and Certification

Keno was enthusiastic and easy to train, and caught on quickly to avalanche search-and-rescue tasks. I only had to show him what to do once, and he'd learn it right away.

The initial training takes about two years. A dog-and-handler team trains daily, and must be tested and reassessed each year to remain actively certified and at peak performance ability. The dog handler has to show that he or she can search a snow avalanche with probes and electronic transceivers, devices that people carry outdoors on mountains to ensure that they can be found quickly under snow. The search-and-rescuer must be a proficient mountain and backcountry skier who is knowledgeable about snowpack structure, avalanche terrain, and how to select the best route for a search. Of course, this person must have all the skills necessary to rescue a victim after finding him or her.

An avalanche search dog needs to respond to basic obedience commands and hand signals. The dog has to have excellent agility and retrieval skills, and needs to be able to search snow avalanches for live victims and articles as well as travel on vehicles with the dog handler.[3]

In avalanche-rescue training sessions, the handler skis up to someone who plays the role of witness to an accident. The witness gives the handler details about what happened. When I'd ski to a witness at a training scenario, there were times when, before I even finished interviewing the witness, Keno had already begun searching or even dug out the first hidden article. He knew the goal and what his job was. From all indications he really liked the work.

Robin's Keno

Another thing I especially appreciated about Keno was that he kept working for as long as an hour without getting tired or bored. I'd give him a break, and he'd go right back to searching again. In this type of job, persistence is essential. Some dogs don't work as long as a half hour before losing interest if they haven't found anything, as if to say, "What are we going to do next?"

In addition to Keno's endurance, he had another essential quality of an avalanche search dog — independence. Although he'd mastered the basic commands of "sit," "stay," "come," "fetch," and "heel" off leash, I didn't demand a high level of obedience from Keno. An avalanche dog needs to be similar to sheepdogs or herding dogs, with a mind of his or her own that doesn't require looking to the handler to figure out everything. Keno had to discern a weak scent from a deeply buried article and sort out how to find it. Although I usually told him which direction to search, I didn't know how he was going to locate, zero in on, and dig up an article. He needed to use his own reasoning and problem-solving skills.

Keno wore a vest when it was time to work. Putting on the vest signaled to him that he had to be 100 percent under my control and couldn't run free. Taking off his collar triggered him to start the search. Knowing he was no longer on leash gave him the idea that he had to start thinking for himself. As the handler, my job was to make sure he covered an entire site. His job was not to miss any scent.

When on a search site, a handler doesn't want the dog to follow him or her around. Instead, the handler tells the dog to go and range over a wide area in a left-to-right direction. The dog must work on his own at a distance from the handler. The dog who can't do this is considered to be "handler bound." A dog who is too well trained in obedience commands might be afraid of getting into trouble for showing initiative. Avalanche search dogs need a strong drive to work on their own.

Like other avalanche search-and-rescue dogs, Keno lived in a kennel. His was at my home, and I gave him attention whenever he did a search. At the end of each training session or rehearsal, the handlers played a big tug-of-war with the dogs. They let the dogs dig up an old, woolen shirt or sweater and play with it. Keno loved when I gave him a new glove that he could rip to shreds. I'd roll around with and pet him, then sit and cuddle with him. I'd give praise by telling him what a great dog he was. After a search or a training exercise, the avalanche rescue dog looks forward to the rewards that follow. The promise of goodies at the end makes searching fun.

Keno was a year or two old by the time we were certified as a senior avalanche-rescue dog team by CARDA in 1998, and received a medal and certificate. Prior to training Keno, I had registered as a dog handler with the Provincial Emergency Program in British Columbia and become a senior CARDA-certified handler. I was an active member of the Fernie Alpine Resort ski-patrol rescue team and worked as its ski-patrol safety supervisor. I also held a valid Standard First Aid certificate.

By the time Keno and I were available for call-out, the dog had no hesitation about being strapped in a harness and lifted into the sky by a helicopter. He didn't fear being loaded onto a ski lift, snowmobile, or snowcat for backcountry and ski-area rescue. Keno had proven that his temperament, discipline, and stability would make him a first-rate avalanche search dog.

We continued our training at Fernie by doing two searches each week, using well-scented, large wool sweaters as hidden articles. We also did live quarry searches in which someone hides in a small snow cave amid avalanche debris in a location unknown to the dog and handler.[4]

Since Fernie gets an average of twenty-nine feet of snow each year — as high as a three-story building — and has five bowls with countless glades, steeps, powder, bumps, and chutes, it's important for the ski-patrol rescue team to be vigilant. On December 20, 2000, just prior to the resort's official opening, I was very grateful that Keno and I had spent the time and effort required to prepare for saving lives.

Keno Makes His First Real Search

The first search Keno and I performed in an actual rescue situation happened on a day when the Fernie Alpine Resort had prepared half the mountain as a safe zone for skiers. We were still doing avalanche control and setup on another part of the mountain. Before the resort opened to the public, the lift operators, who worked for the patrol, were given designated routes to take.

Twenty-one-year-old Ryan Radchenko was working his first day on his new job as lift operator at the top of the White Pass chairlift. He had misinterpreted the instructions and thought that, while on break, he could use any ski run instead of merely the designated safe route.

Ryan had done carpentry at Fernie that summer. In the fall, I had brought Keno to work one day and happened to introduce him to Ryan, who had held out his hand to Keno and said, "Keno, get a good sniff. You never know what may happen. You may have to rescue me this winter." We had all laughed at the comment, because a dog doesn't dig up a person from remembering that person; the dog is trained to find any human scent.

On this day, when Keno would be called to rescue Ryan, the young man traversed onto an avalanche slope that had been blasted that morning. Two patrollers, Dave Richards and Paul Wright, were crossing the slope when Ryan skied up to twenty feet below them. The patrollers asked, "What are you doing there? Why are you going for a run in the closed area? Come with us. We'll get you out of here."

Dave asked Ryan if he had an avalanche transceiver on. He didn't.

Just as Dave said, "You need to come with us," the slope broke underneath the young man, and a thundering wave of snow pushed him down the mountain. Dave skied quickly off the avalanche. Horrified, the two patrollers watched, while the snow, as compact as wet concrete, swept Ryan one to two hundred meters. Ryan disappeared into a cloud of snow that held him in its grip. Although Ryan fought to stay on top of the snow, the avalanche buried him eight feet beneath the surface, at the bottom of the slope, somewhere underneath the chairlift.

After Dave and Paul called in the emergency, the ski-patrol dispatcher alerted all patrollers to the accident site. I heard the news of an avalanche burial confirmed on my radio. It troubled me that Ryan did not have a transceiver, making this situation even more dangerous.

Before heading to the slope, I called for someone from the maintenance department to bring Keno from the base on a snowmobile.

I got onto the ski lift and rode it to the top of the avalanche, feeling scared and pessimistic about finding Ryan under these circumstances. If we didn't locate him soon, he would die. As soon as his air supply ran out, he would suffocate from asphyxiation by breathing his own carbon dioxide. Also, he might be severely injured from hitting trees or rocks as the fast-moving avalanche hurtled him down the mountain.

When I arrived at the site where Ryan was buried, Sue Boyd and Keno's mother were already there. I could see ten to fifteen searchers randomly probing and working with shovels. It wasn't a huge area, only about an acre of deposit, but its width presented a big challenge for quickly finding a body. We started poking holes in the snowpack so the scent could rise and make it easier for the dogs to find Ryan.

By the time I arrived, Ryan had been buried for fifteen minutes. I knew the snow was swiftly transforming into an icy tomb with no way for light and air to reach him. I still had to wait for Keno's arrival. Time was running out. The search dogs would soon become Ryan's last hope for survival.

I was relieved to see my dog running up to me over the top of the avalanche after the lift-maintenance person brought Keno on a snowmobile. I immediately took off his collar and commanded, "Search, Keno."

We split up the area with the other avalanche search-dog team. Keno began air-scenting and covering the site. He snuffled his nose into the snow. It had now been over twenty-two minutes since the avalanche.

I was torn between continuing to probe and keeping an eye on Keno. I saw him start frantically digging into an area of solidly packed snow. In less than two minutes, Keno pulled up Ryan's glove. He had ripped it off Ryan's hand, which was sticking up beneath a little over a foot of snow. The young man had had the presence of mind to push his arm toward the snow's surface before starting to lose consciousness. His head was underneath the snow with his body one and a half meters down.

I ran over to where Keno stood with the glove in his mouth and reached for Ryan's extended hand. It felt limp and lifeless in mine.

I shouted for the other searchers to join me. Looking over my shoulder and sticking his sniffing nose into the group as far as possible, Keno watched with eagerness. I started digging straight down as quickly as possible. I had to reach Ryan fast and get air to him before his body shut down completely.

As I dug closer to his head and uncovered it, I could see that Ryan was unconscious. I yelled, "He's alive and breathing!" Although he still had color in his face, it was impossible to tell if he would make it. His eyes were open but unblinking, with constricted pupils. I couldn't tell if his legs had bent back under his head or if his body had been crushed into some other fatal contortion. His temperature might have dropped, leaving him hypothermic.

In the first moments after I did emergency first aid, Ryan remained unconscious but breathed in response to the oxygen therapy. Now I knew he would survive.

By the time we pulled Ryan out of the snow and slid a spinal board under him, he had been buried for close to twenty-five minutes. We skied Ryan on the board down the hill to an ambulance that waited to take him to the hospital.

A Happy Ending for Everyone

An astonishing fact began to sink in: we had made our first live find. Keno had saved Ryan's life. The extensive CARDA training enables us to pull off a rescue so that everything occurs in a practical sequence. Although I'd trained for years, I didn't think finding someone alive would happen to me, but I sure was glad when it worked out that way.

The happy ending of this rescue came about when Ryan returned to Fernie from the hospital only a half hour later. By then, he knew that Keno had saved his life. He was very appreciative and thanked all the patrol handlers and search dogs, especially Keno. He was shaken but talking and ready to go back to work to finish his shift. We sent him home for the day anyway. He continued to work at Fernie for a few more years.

CARDA was thrilled to have one of its certified dog handlers make the organization's first live rescue. In fact, this was the first live find by an avalanche rescue dog in Canada. To celebrate, the CARDA officers planned to take Keno for a steak dinner at the best restaurant in town, but the place didn't allow dogs. Instead, that night they brought over a ten-ounce sirloin steak. I cooked it rare for

Keno, the way he liked it, and gave my brave and intelligent dog his well-deserved reward.

The reality of this situation was that if Keno hadn't found Ryan alive, I would have been held responsible. It was my job to keep everyone safe while they were on the mountain. I would have had to answer for why a staff person got killed. Instead, I spent two months on the phone talking to media about the good news of Keno's live find. I would have spent two years under investigation had it gone the other way.

Work continued for Keno and me. We were called to quite a few recoveries after our first actual search. We helped locate victims, but the subsequent searches all had tragic outcomes.

Each year, on the anniversary of saving her son's life, Ryan's mother brought a steak for Keno and a bottle of Jägermeister for the ski patrol as gifts of gratitude.

Keno, the Publicity Hound

For a couple of months after finding Ryan, Keno's rescue became a good public relations and news story for Fernie Alpine Resort, especially since it happened right before Christmas. Keno didn't really know what was going on, but he was photogenic and didn't mind having his picture taken.

In February, people from the television program *Animal Miracles* came here to produce a show segment about the rescue.[5] They did a fantastic job of capturing what went on without sensationalizing the event and the amount of risk involved.

During the reenactment, Keno had a strange expression on his face. He knew whether or not a victim was okay. While everyone was digging out one of the patrollers, who pretended to be underneath an avalanche, Keno looked as if he thought, "Why is everybody working on this guy? There's nothing the matter here."

In 2002 Keno and I were flown to Toronto for a ceremony in which Keno was inducted into the Purina Animal Hall of Fame. Keno was the first non–police dog to receive the Service Dog of the Year award.[6]

Keno Retires

At the mountain where I work, we have an avalanche rescue program with two certified dogs on the staff. I started the job I have now, as mountain operations manager, and realized that it came with increased responsibilities. This meant I didn't have time to train and keep Keno active. We continued search-and-rescue work for about a year, and he stayed at the required proficiency level. But, since other dogs were capable of covering the zone, I decided to let Keno have a more leisurely lifestyle in his aging years. In 2004 he retired.

Retirement turned out to be good for Keno and for my family. He changed from living in the kennel to becoming our pet. He slept in my son's bed. He played tug-of-war to his heart's content.

On St. Patrick's Day 2007, Keno died of natural causes. He was eleven and a half years old. My son and I buried Keno in a gravesite with a wooden cross marker that contained an imprint of his paw print. A photo of his golden, furry face shows his wide, brown eyes gazing out over the snowy mountains he loved so much. Keno was a really pleasant dog with good manners, and I miss him.

He was the success story that made all the training worthwhile.

His live find became an inspiration for the whole CARDA organization. Keno represents something I got into merely as an interest that allowed me to meet the supportive people from CARDA and Hini Maleau from the German Avalanche Rescue Dog Association. They taught me how to teach my dog. It was as if all the instructors and dog handlers formed the structure of a pyramid with Keno's live find at the pyramid's tip. Keno's action provided a culmination for the entire CARDA organization to show what it is capable of doing.

Ryan owes Keno his life. And so do I. He truly was a wonder dog.

MEDITATION

Keno's endurance and independence made him outstanding at giving service for avalanche victims. What innate qualities do you have for fulfilling your life's purpose?

The Dogs Who Taught Me
How Amazing Dogs Can Be

Bonita M. Bergin, PhD
Santa Rosa, California

*D*ogs are phenomenal, and our ancient relationships with them intrigue me. When it comes to dogs, I'm more of a scientist than a warm enthusiast. I don't try to make them into something they are not. Yet I have grown to experience dogs as amazing, intelligent, and empathetic, as well as having an awesome sense of responsibility.

I teach classes at the Bergin University of Canine Studies, the only college offering associate's, bachelor's, and master's degrees in Human-Canine Life Sciences and Assistance-Dog Education. We are working on becoming accredited. In my classes, I demonstrate how similar dogs are to humans. There is more than a 75 percent overlap between humans and canines in genetic coding. My goal is to help our students teach in ways that give dogs the opportunity to expand their remarkable minds.

I share stories with my students about a series of incredible dogs who have given me firsthand experience with what dogs can be and do.

Abdul, the First Service Dog

After returning with my husband, Jim, from teaching in Australia and Turkey in 1974, I started working toward a master's degree in special education. I had lingering impressions of animals, such as burros and donkeys, assisting people with disabilities in countries where I had traveled. As part of my special education studies, I joined a master's program in which students discussed ways to help people with disabilities become more self-sufficient. Burros and donkeys wouldn't be feasible as helpers in the Western world, but it occurred to me that dogs might be able to assist. In those days no one realized dogs could become indispensable companions for people with disabilities.

I went to an organization that trained dogs to lead blind people around obstacles and alert them to street curbs and traffic. I presented my idea that people with disabilities, even those in wheelchairs, should have dogs who could assist them. The people who manage dog guides for the blind said that what I wanted to do couldn't be done.

When I approached regular dog trainers about the concept of dogs assisting people with disabilities, they also said it couldn't be done. Dog training in the early seventies mainly consisted of choke-chain jerks and fear techniques. All the aversive methods were about training a dog's body, not his mind. Everyone assumed that because people with disabilities had no strength to hold on to a leash, give a choke-chain jerk, or bring a misbehaving dog back into line, dogs would be too unruly for them to handle.

I finally decided that if I couldn't find anyone else to implement my idea, I would do it myself. I started calling around to organizations and asking if someone with a disability might be interested in having a dog assist him or her. One call I made was to a program called Community Resources for Independence (CRI). When I described my idea to the woman who answered the phone, she said, "I'll do it."

The young woman I talked to that day was Kerrill (Kerry) Knaus, a nineteen-year-old quadriplegic who was severely disabled with muscular dystrophy. If Kerry's head fell forward onto her chest, she didn't have the muscles in her neck or arm to lift or push it back up, and needed someone to do this for her. She was only able to hold the equivalent of an ounce in each hand and could move very little, with minimal range of motion. She used a power wheelchair to get around. (Kerry tells about her experiences as the first person with physical disabilities to have a service dog in the story that follows mine in this book.)

At that time I had a very sweet, gentle female golden retriever named Jada who came into heat. One day Jim took Jada out to toilet in our backyard. I'd told him to always stay with her, but he appeared in our doorway without the dog. With a note of panic in my voice, I asked, "Where's Jada?"

He said, "Oh, there aren't any dogs around."

I went running out the door to find Jada being bred by a Labrador retriever.

Jada's accidental first litter was born around the same time Kerry and I had agreed to work together with a dog. Jim and I kept one little black puppy from Jada's litter for us. The puppy was a mix of lovable Lab from his father, who gave the dog his black coloring, and the gentleness of a golden retriever from his mother. I thought his personality and intelligence might be a good match for Kerry.

All my life I'd had pet dogs and loved them dearly. But I knew nothing about formally training them and had not worked with people with disabilities. I naively thought that if the dog lived with and got to know Kerry well, he would learn about her disability, and everything would work out fine.

A puppy isn't easy to manage though, and Kerry's attendants wouldn't accept responsibility for the dog. Since people with disabilities are dependent on attendants for their needs, it would have been risky for Kerry to go against her attendants' wishes. Later, as the love deepened between Kerry and the dog, and she came to rely on him more, she insisted that he live with her. Her attendants adjusted to the situation and eventually came to appreciate the dog's help. However, at first I had to keep the puppy with me to do the initial teaching. I took the dog to meet with Kerry regularly, and she worked with him too. After she adopted him, Kerry named the dog Abdul.

We started our work with my attaching Abdul's leash to Kerry's power wheelchair and teaching him to sit and lie down. He was a very responsive and incredibly special dog who did everything we asked him to do. Abdul had a fair degree of energy but not too much. He was gracious, kind, and willing to pay attention to Kerry, even though her voice and body — unlike her personality and determination — were very weak. When she and Abdul connected, it was just magic. Kerry was able to follow through on giving the commands I had taught Abdul, and he obeyed her.

As we progressed, I asked Kerry, "How could Abdul help in your life?"

Kerry said, "When I sit in the living room and my attendant

leaves in the middle of the afternoon to go grocery shopping, sometimes it's dark before she returns. This means I'm left in the dark alone. I'd like the dog to be able to turn the light on for me."

So we taught Abdul how to turn on Kerry's lights.

Then Kerry said, "One attendant leaves lunch in a sack in the refrigerator. The next attendant gives me the lunch. But sometimes that attendant comes late, and I don't get anything to eat. So I would like the dog to tug open the refrigerator door, retrieve the sack lunch, and put the bag on my wheelchair shelf. Then I can very carefully and slowly open the bag and get out the sandwich."

So we taught Abdul how to retrieve Kerry's lunch from the refrigerator and bring it to her wheelchair tray table.

Kerry (Kerrill) and Abdul

Kerry said, "I drop things all the time. I want the dog to pick them up and bring them back to me." She also explained that if there were a fire or she wanted to get some fresh air, she would have no way to open the door.

We taught Abdul to pick up items Kerry dropped and to tug open the door to her double-wide mobile home.

Abdul wanted nothing more than to please Kerry, and at the same time he had such a joyful personality. He listened and cared. With her very soft voice and physical weakness, she had no way of correcting him, but he still tried to figure out what she needed and provide it. Kerry and Abdul loved each other through a fifteen-year relationship. Although she has had service dogs since Abdul, she treasures the role he played in transforming her life.

Abdul's determination and ability made it possible for my dream of teaching dogs to assist people with disabilities become a reality. Without Abdul, service dogs for people with disabilities could not have evolved in the way and at the time that it did.

Founding Canine Companions for Independence

Even after Abdul showed me that a dog could be taught to assist people with disabilities beyond what was being done for the blind and deaf, I was trying to give the idea away. All I wanted to do was keep teaching. There was no question in my mind that the job had to be done. So when I couldn't find anybody else, I continued to develop the project by trial and error. In 1978 I founded Canine Companions for Independence (CCI) as a nonprofit organization. In the next decade of my involvement with the organization, CCI moved out of my home and grew into having a national office, four regional training centers, a paid staff of sixty-five people, and a $3 million yearly budget.

I came up with the name *service dog* for the concept of dogs who help people with disabilities other than the blind and deaf. I also taught dogs to assist deaf people and called them *signal dogs*. This term is still used in the California state law stipulating that signal dogs can accompany deaf people everywhere. I used the generally accepted term *social-therapy dog* for when volunteers teach their own dogs to socialize with people in nursing homes and hospitals; sometimes such visits are even written into the patient's treatment plan.

I continued trying to determine what breed or breeds would

have the right temperament and health to become good service dogs with a strong willingness to please. I eventually started selecting dogs with low levels of arousal, less initiative, and low-level predatory instincts to breed as service dogs. This type of dog, usually a golden or Labrador retriever, doesn't have a strong drive to chase cats. The breed also doesn't try to figure things out on his own but waits to be told what to do. It's very hard to train low-arousal dogs, because they don't easily get energized about doing the task. But once they learn something, it stays with them forever. This ability to remember what they are taught is one characteristic that makes service dogs unique. All along the way of learning what traits service dogs needed, the dogs always taught me.

The people with disabilities told me amazing stories about what their service dogs did to help. I didn't believe them at first and thought they must have exaggerated or that the dog had done something exceptional by accident. I didn't understand then, as I do now, that dogs have the kind of mind that is capable of sophisticated thinking, analyzing, and problem solving.

Teaching Service Dogs

Even though my techniques worked with Abdul and other dogs after him, I didn't trust my knowledge and decided that I needed to focus on administration at CCI and hire professional trainers. I knew that I didn't have their award-winning experience in training and showing dogs. The professionals did a beautiful job, and our dogs looked fabulous. But after the dogs graduated and were placed, for the first time I started getting calls that the service dogs weren't working out.

I didn't know at the time that we were experiencing a phenomenon called *context-dependent learning*. This means that something needs to be taught in the context in which it will be applied. The professionals had trained the dogs with choke-chain jerks to get them to do tasks. Then, when the dogs were placed with clients who couldn't use those techniques, these crafty canines thought, "Aha, I don't have to do those jobs after all." I have had many epiphanies over the years, and this was one of them: dogs stop responding if they aren't doing the service out of love. I started throwing out other people's methods and went back to my own ways of teaching the dogs. Our service dogs operate as thinking, caring, and responsive individuals.

Teaching with our methods taps into their immense capabilities. Now I know that when we teach the mind of a dog, his body will follow. Successful methods for teaching children — praise, enthusiasm, and clear instructions — enhance a dog's ability to learn. When dogs are *taught* instead of *trained*, they develop a strong bond with the teacher. A service dog who is taught through respectful methods makes a positive transition to helping a person with a disability with whom he is matched. The dog has learned to trust that there will be love in his life.

Teaching Dogs to Read

When I first started teaching dogs, I incrementally became more aware that their cognition was significantly deeper than I had been led to believe. I began to wonder whether dogs could learn to read. Dogs who read could communicate important information to us.

For example, if a dog guide for the blind could read the word indicating an exit sign, he could lead his blind person to it in order to leave the shopping mall. A reading dog could find the symbols that indicate which restroom to use — male, female, or handicapped. At anyone's home, a reading dog could be taught to recognize the symbol Ø and know that those brownies with the Ø sign in front of them on the table are off-limits.

I like to speculate about what the process of recognizing written words and symbols could do for the dogs themselves. In my book *Teach Your Dog to Read*, I wrote, "Reading stimulates networking between different parts of the brain, and networking enhances the ability to conceptualize. Although I haven't met any canine Einsteins, it's possible that reading can likewise expand a dog's mind so that he is capable of more thinking and problem solving. Who knows where their growing minds will take us? Dogs who can read are dogs of the future."[7]

I started by showing pictures to the dogs. They did so well with picture identification that it got boring, so I switched to having them read stick figures. Later on, I learned that recognizing pictures and responding to them was even more cognitively advanced than reading stick figures.

A service assistance dog knows how to do ninety commands. We teach all of our dogs to read the basic obedience commands, such as "sit," "down," "roll," or "turn." Some of our clients have taught their dogs to read as many as twenty of those written commands. We haven't seen that here yet, but we now have six to eight words that our dogs can read.

The Dogs Who Prove How Smart Dogs Can Be

In 1991, I left CCI to found the Assistance Dog Institute (ADI), where we teach our students how to train service dogs and match them to people with disabilities. At ADI we are always learning more about what dogs can do. Our offices have Dutch doors with doorknobs that are not round but have a flap that sticks out. The dogs open them all the time. We're always in trouble from having taught these dogs so well. We must come up with clever ways to stop them from doing things they can figure out easily.

Rather than keep the dogs in kennels, we have them stay with us in our offices. They are with people all the time. We had one dog who would open the office door, go around the corner and open the hallway door, go around the next corner and open the workroom door, open one of the offices in the workroom, and join the dogs in that office. I guess he wanted to have a party. When he was finished visiting, he would leave the workroom office, close the door, and let himself back into the office where he was supposed to stay.

Keila Remembers

My dog Keila looked very much like Abdul. I adopted her from the pound. Her former family had tied her to a tree all day, and neighborhood children threw rocks at her. At night the family let Keila go free to forage for food. She'd come back in the morning, and they'd tie her up again. I knew about her history but didn't realize what cognitive skills she had mastered as a result of having to survive.

One time I was throwing a tennis ball for our six dogs, and it landed in the middle of our swimming pool on top of the pool's bubble covering. All my dogs knew not to step on the bubble cover, because it would sink into the pool under their weight.

In search of the ball I had thrown, several of the dogs, including Keila, ran to the edge of the swimming pool. They worked in concert, like a team, by grabbing the cover's edges, backing up, holding it in their mouths, then repeating the movements until they had pulled the tennis ball, still on top of the cover, to the side of the pool. Even though the cover was now on solid ground, they continued to assume that they would fall in the pool if they stepped on it.

Bonnie's Keila

I pushed the cover onto the pool again and figured the game was over. I looked back to see that Keila had squatted on the edge of the swimming pool. With her front paws she accordion-pleated the cover, creating one fold after another until the ball inched over to her. Without having to step on the cover, she plucked the ball off it and walked away. I was so astounded at the skill it had taken for Keila to do this that I taught about her in my class for several years.

Three years later, I wondered if Keila could do this tennis-ball trick again. I threw the ball for my dogs in the backyard, and it landed on the bubble cover. Keila did the accordion pleating of the cover and retrieved the ball. She had strategized how to do it all those years ago and still remembered. That's the kind of brilliant mind these dogs have.

Hoja Does the Right Thing

Hoja was an Anatolian shepherd who belonged to Jim and me. Anatolian shepherds are not easily trainable dogs. They're bred to stay outdoors with sheep or goats on the Anatolian plateau in Turkey and guard the livestock. Unlike a golden retriever or Lab, they're not warm, friendly, and fuzzy. I had taught Hoja all the service-dog commands, but she would only do them for food, never merely to please me. *Hoja* is a Turkish name for "teacher," and this is the dog who taught me that dogs have consciences.

Bonnie and Hoja

One of the skills we teach all our dogs is to alert their companions. The dog will come and tap a person on the leg or hand so that she knows that the dog needs to show her something. As soon as a dog gives the alert tap, the human is supposed to respond by saying, "What?" The dog will look the person in the eye and walk her to whatever he wants her to know. Sometimes he wants to draw the person's attention to the refrigerator for food or to the back door when he needs to go outside.

I occasionally brought a puppy home for a visit. Hoja wasn't happy about visitors and barely tolerated them. One day I took a little puppy named Helen home. That day I was feeling exceptionally tired. Hoja was in the front yard. I parked the car, took Helen out of it, and locked the pup in the front yard inside the fenced-in area that spans both the front yard and the backyard. Then I walked into the house with Hoja. The swimming pool was located in the backyard.

I plopped down on the couch, thinking, "Okay, I have at least three minutes before that puppy will get to the backyard."

I had barely sat down when Hoja walked over and started nosing me, alerting. Of course, I knew this meant that I had to get up and follow her. But I thought, "Do I really have to do this right now? Can I wait a couple of minutes?" But I had always taught my students that when the dog says to follow, you have to do it, or he will stop believing or trusting that you'll respond.

Finally I stood up. Hoja slowly walked to the sliding glass door that opened to the backyard. I looked outside and saw Helen in the swimming pool. It had happened so fast that the puppy must have run around from the front yard as soon as I left her there.

In spite of the fact that Hoja would have been just as happy for that intruding puppy to drown, she knew that I would have been sad. Although Hoja did what came naturally to a livestock guard dog by alerting and taking me to save the puppy, I believe that she also acted ethically and morally. I think that's a stunning thing.

At-Risk Teens Teach Service Dogs

In ADI's High-School Assistance-Dog program we work with at-risk teens to train them to teach service dogs for people with disabilities. In 2001 our program won Oprah Winfrey's Use Your Life Award.

Whether they are in juvenile detention centers, residential group homes, or alternative education programs, these teens learn emotional self-control and the importance of positive reinforcement by teaching dogs. Instead of hitting or knocking somebody around, which was how many of them were raised, they're giving treats to the dogs, being kind and loving, and finding out that rewards work well. One of our goals is to use the dogs to help the teens feel loved. Often their moms and dads might be in prison, or there are drugs and alcohol in the home. Consequently the teens haven't been given enough attention and don't feel loved.

For ten years we have taken our dogs to the juvenile hall. It is a special moment when the dogs excitedly run up to the teens who've been teaching them. The kids are also thrilled to greet their dogs. By having the dogs help break their cycle of abuse, the teens no longer feel as if they have to beat up somebody. Instead they can have a respectful, affectionate relationship without violence or manipulation. The dogs bring these kids love and a sense of belonging.

The kids must develop emotional self-control to work with the dogs, and this skill stays with them long after graduation. They come back to see us and tell how the program turned their lives around and what a huge difference it has made, especially in parenting skills. Teaching the dogs enables them to experience a whole different way of life. And as adults, they all love their family dogs, which is another big benefit of the program.

Dogs have a positive effect on both kids and adults, and we now have the statistics to prove it. On the days we are in the high school, the percentage of school attendance increases overall. When the dogs are at school, calls for police to handle problems decrease. The staff, faculty, and kids say they are happier on days when the dogs are present.

Little did we know that when Abdul became Kerry's caring and loving service dog, he would start an international movement to aid people with disabilities and also become the catalyst for studying dogs and what they are capable of doing. I am so thankful for Abdul. I don't know what would have happened without him. I don't know if I would have given up. The many dogs who have followed in his paw prints have led the way for all of us to marvel at the immensity of a dog's heart and mind.

MEDITATION

What behavior have you observed in a dog that seemed to go far beyond instinct to reveal a sentient, conscious being?

Abdul, the History-Making Service Dog

Kerrill Knaus-Hardy
Scotts Mills, Oregon

*W*hile I was volunteering to answer the phone at Community Resources for Independence (CRI), in Santa Rosa, California, in 1976, Bonnie (Bonita) Bergin called. She was looking for someone to experiment with her to find out if dogs could help people with disabilities.

At first, I thought she was crazy. She didn't seem to have a clear idea of what the dogs would be doing. Besides, prior to Bonnie's request, I'd had a couple of strange calls that day, so I didn't take her seriously. After we talked longer and the conversation progressed, even though she wasn't sure which direction to take, I had a better idea of what Bonnie wanted to do. I recognized that dogs helping people with physical disabilities could potentially be a good idea.

I was a country girl who'd had dogs as pets and loved them. Even though I've had muscular dystrophy all my life and use a power wheelchair to get around, I was in 4-H and worked with horses, sheep, and other animals. Having a supportive family, a love of nature, and beloved animals had helped me live an adventurous life so far. But one of my biggest adventures was about to start with Bonnie Bergin's phone call. Only I didn't know it yet.

After I began to understand what Bonnie wanted to do, I referred her to my boss at CRI, a man with disabilities whom I thought would work well for the project. He called me at home that night and said he was sending Bonnie back to me. He had even given her my home telephone number. Bonnie called me right away that

Kerrill and Abdul

same night. She was so diligent that I finally said yes to the experiment, and she immediately brought Abdul over to my home. Anybody who knows Bonnie would agree that she's tenacious. Later, I was very glad she had persisted with me.

After Bonnie placed a Labrador–golden retriever mixed-breed puppy with me and we started working together, I had to quickly give this little bundle of energy a name. Some friends and I sat around together one night, drinking beer, having fun, and looking through the white pages of the phone book. The name Abdul caught my eye. Later, I learned that it was perfect for the puppy. In Moroccan Arabic the name means *black*, and Abdul had a lustrous ebony coat. But even more appropriate, in standard Arabic, Abdul means *servant* or *helper*. Combined with Allah, as in Abdullah, it means *servant of God*.

Abdul's Growing Pains

I had worked with Bonnie for a couple months when I took a summer vacation to Oregon to spend time with my family. Because I had attendants who didn't want the hassle or responsibility of caring for both a puppy and me, so far it was best that Bonnie keep Abdul with her. I thought he was more attached to her than to me. I decided to take the puppy with me to Oregon in hopes that we would bond better by having more concentrated time together.

After having Abdul with me constantly for the two-week vacation, I really began to appreciate what an amazing dog he was. Because until that time I hadn't thought I could keep him with me, I had resolved not to get too close emotionally. After I returned home from vacation though, I told my attendants, "Abdul is staying here." Eventually they grew accustomed to the dog. And after all, attendants come and go. Abdul would be my companion for the next fifteen years.

It took about a year before Abdul could work for me in ways that were useful. I raised him from just a tiny guy, and he was every bit the obnoxious, annoying puppy. He was curious and enormously energetic. He chewed up everything when I had to leave him at home to go to work or school. I didn't know how to confine him, so every day he trashed my house. He taught me and I learned that I had nothing of value except him.

After hearing about all the damage the puppy was causing, my family didn't think it was such a good idea for him to live with me. When they found out that he had chewed up my family's Bible, they grew even more resentful and tried to talk me into giving Abdul back to Bonnie.

I'm pretty stubborn though. I had been living on my own, not at my family's home, and was proving that I could handle being independent. I wasn't about to let anyone tell me that I could or couldn't have a dog. But at one point my mom told me that I was welcome to come home for another visit but couldn't bring the dog. I said, "Well, I guess I won't be seeing you then."

Amazing Abdul

After a while, my mother realized that if she ever wanted to see me again, she would have to let my dog come with me. This is how I wound up making the second visit to Oregon with Abdul a couple of years later. By then, he was very well trained, but my family had never seen him work. It was the mid-seventies, and there was no such thing as a service dog for people with physical disabilities. My family couldn't have imagined what Abdul was like, because they had no firsthand experience with such a concept.

On this visit my family had to leave me at home while they went into town to run errands. Unexpectedly they were delayed in returning, because the errands took longer than they had anticipated. It started to get dark. With no cell phones or any way of checking on me, they became very concerned.

For my whole life, whenever people were gone too long, without anyone at home to turn on the lights, I'd have to sit in my wheelchair and watch the room dim and fade to black as the sun set. Naturally my family was worried about poor Kerry being stuck in the dark while they were in town.

When they returned home this time though, they found me sitting in the house with all the lights on, watching television. I had also eaten dinner. With great satisfaction I asked, "Why were you worried? I had Abdul turn on the lights and give me the television remote control. He opened the refrigerator and brought me some food." With this, they were actually seeing a service dog in action, performing practical tasks. That day marked the end of any objections they'd had to Abdul. He had won them over.

While I was in Oregon, my family arranged for me to speak to a support group run by a therapist for people who were newly disabled. This was the first time my mother ever saw me give a demonstration with Abdul and speak about him. The attendees at my talk were amazed when I showed them what Abdul could do for me. He knew how to operate elevator buttons, accompany me to college classes while carrying my filled backpack, place himself precisely in different positions so I could reach compartments in my backpack, turn on my car heater, open doors, switch on lights, and give me the remote for my wheelchair lift if I dropped it.

I continued the presentation by answering questions from newly injured people. Everyone became so excited that what was supposed to be a twenty-minute talk lasted ninety minutes. People wouldn't leave. They wanted to know more about how to get a dog like Abdul to help them. At that time there were no laws for access, and it was unheard of to have a service-dog assistant.

My family was amazed at the significance of what they witnessed. They could see these people clamoring for the same independence I was experiencing. My mom was speechless. Tears filled her eyes. Afterward, Mom said, "I had no idea. I'm so glad you went through with this and didn't listen to us."

My mom is as stubborn and independent as Bonnie and I. But she admitted that she had been wrong and apologized to me for the first time I could remember. Since then, she has become one of my biggest advocates. When Bonnie founded Canine Companions for Independence (CCI), my mother helped to find an attorney to incorporate it as a nonprofit organization. She served on the CCI board and talked about CCI and its programs with everybody she met in business or socially. To anyone who would listen, she raved about Abdul and what he had done for me.

Why Abdul Was the Right Dog for the Job

Abdul had four important characteristics that made him such a successful helper to me. First, he was extremely intelligent. This was why he was such a difficult puppy to raise. Very intelligent dogs can be a real pain in the butt, because their humans can't manage them. The dog can outsmart the person. Abdul was as good at figuring out how to get what he wanted as he was at learning how to do new things. He could manipulate his way out of just about anything. Less-intelligent dogs lie around and wait for you to help them. A bright dog like Abdul figures things out for himself.

Second, as he grew up, his motivation changed from finding how to achieve his own goals to becoming extremely loyal and dedicated. He transformed into a dog who tried to understand what I needed and how to help me.

Third, Abdul excelled so much at being attuned to my needs that some people thought he had psychic powers. He could anticipate what I would ask before I asked it, and we worked together harmoniously. An observer couldn't tell that I was giving Abdul commands. Everything looked automatic. After he matured, I no longer needed to give him direct commands. He grew to know me as well as I knew him.

Fourth, Abdul had the ability to link things together and perform tasks he had never been taught to do. He could strategize and try different approaches to solving problems. This is rare in a dog.

An example of Abdul's skill at resolving complicated problems by processing information happened when he was only five months old. There was a large pillow that belonged to my roommate in the living room of our apartment. Abdul thought it was a wonderful pillow — soft, squishy, big, and warm. My roommate would tell Abdul to get off the pillow. It was her floor pillow for people to lounge on, not a dog bed, and Abdul wasn't her dog. Why should she put up with having dog hair on her pillow?

In addition to lying on her reserved pillow, Abdul also loved to sit in the kitchen and watch my roommate cook so he could grab anything that might fall on the floor. Because of his skill at swooping up food, I had taught him the command, "Get out of the kitchen." Of course, he also had learned the command, "Get off the pillow." In addition, he knew many other commands, such as "walk," "sit," and "lie down."

One day Abdul was in the kitchen, getting in my roommate's way. She turned to him and hurled a string of commands: "Get out of the kitchen. Go in the living room. Lie down on the pillow."

Abdul had only been told to *get off* the pillow, not to *lie on* the pillow. Except for this one command, he had been taught all the other things my roommate told him to do but in a different order. Yet he did exactly what she commanded in the correct order. He left the kitchen, went into the living room, and plopped down on the pillow.

Abdul Never Stopped Loving

From fall 1988 through summer 1989 I was on a scholarship in Canada. I had gone there with Abdul to study horse training and teaching techniques for what I'm doing now with my Adaptive Riding Institute. Winter in Toronto is frigidly cold. By this time, Abdul had been diagnosed with bone cancer. I knew he did not have much longer to live. The cold weather bothered him and worsened the effects of his cancer.

I talked to Joy, a friend of mine who lives in San Diego. After me, Joy was Abdul's best friend. Abdul loved Joy so much that whenever she came to visit me, once he made sure I was settled in my bedroom, instead of sleeping with me as he normally did, he went to sleep in the bedroom with Joy.

I feared that I'd have to put Abdul to sleep prematurely, because the Canadian winter caused him so much pain. Since I was obligated to be there for my scholarship, Joy agreed to bring Abdul to San Diego, where he would be warm, comfortable, and spoiled. Knowing how much he loved Joy, I was happy for him to have a good place to live while I finished my studies.

Joy called me from San Diego with regular reports. Abdul was doing great. She gave him pain medication. He got to play in her house and lie in the sun. In contrast I was in a bind, living in a foreign country and in inaccessible housing without my dog. I'd had a dog since I was eighteen years old. For the first time in all these years, I felt like a handicapped person.

After Abdul left Canada, I went through an emergency situation in which I could have died. I had forgotten about my inability to open doors by myself and made my way across campus in a snowstorm only to find out that the class had been canceled. I couldn't get into the building and had to sit in my wheelchair out in -12°C weather until someone came along and let me inside. That's when I decided that this was stupid. It was critical that I get a dog right away.

I talked to Bonnie, and she found a replacement dog for me. Petunia had finished training but not yet officially graduated from Bonnie's latest class. Bonnie made arrangements to send the dog to me in Canada immediately.

On December 7, 1988, I was on my way to the airport to pick up Petunia, who was being flown to Toronto. I remember sitting in my van when suddenly, even though Abdul and I were separated by thousands of miles, a wave of total awareness rushed through me. I knew that Abdul had died in that moment.

After I returned home with Petunia, the phone rang and I knew it was Joy calling to tell me of Abdul's passing. I asked, "What time was it?" Her answer confirmed that Abdul had left this world exactly when I had sensed that he was gone.

Joy said that in the days prior to his death, Abdul had felt good. His medications had been working well. He had been eating and playing just fine. But that morning, he had refused to eat. He didn't want to get up and wouldn't walk. As I continued to question Joy, it became clear that Abdul had stopped eating at exactly the time that Bonnie put Petunia on the flight to Toronto. I believe that Abdul knew that his responsibility to me had ended. Our connection was so strong that it surpassed distance, space, and time. He quit trying to live when his replacement was on the way. It was as if he knew it would be okay to leave.

I can't explain why it happened that way other than the strong connection the years we spent together had formed. It was pretty amazing. Abdul knew. And I knew.

The three dogs who followed Abdul all did fine jobs, but he remained the most uniquely gifted. Because I was so young when I got him and all of this was new to me, I thought that I was remembering Abdul's service with more awe and magic than had really occurred. Finally, after the third dog I had to accept that there would never be another dog like Abdul. It was like a first kiss; over time, fantasy makes the moment greater. Maybe I was remembering Abdul as being smarter than he was and that's why no other dog could match up to him.

But Nancy, the eight-year-old yellow-Lab and golden-retriever cross I have now, is much like Abdul in how she thinks and processes information. Her emotional makeup is similar to his too. I'm really shocked to find that, in essence, she is almost a clone of Abdul. She is not as intelligent as he was but has the same degree of devotion, loyalty, and willingness. It's exciting and wonderful to discover that I can have that relationship again with another dog, the right dog.

Abdul earned the honor and had the distinction of being the first service dog raised by and for a person with physical disabilities who was able to implement Bonnie's training procedures. His mission and legacy live on in every service dog who has come after him.

MEDITATION

Has a dog enabled you to be the first to give service? Could you find a way to serve life that fulfills your noble purpose?

CHAPTER TWO

A Mission to Inspire

We all hunger for more in life, consciously or unconsciously. Some of us may not be aware of this hunger or may only sense it in rare moments of consciousness, but it's there.

— Judith Wright

The Littlest Police Dog in the World

Sheriff Dan McClelland
Chardon, Ohio

*T*he *Guinness World Records 2008* has a new entry in it. Midge, my Chihuahua–rat terrier mix, is listed as the world's smallest police dog. Midge gets publicity and fan letters from around the world. She has been featured in newspaper and magazine articles and was on British television. *Life* magazine did an article with photos. A national news magazine in China featured Midge's story. I've done interviews for a Canadian radio station and one in Chicago. When people ask me how Midge handles all the publicity, I say, "She can't read, and I don't let her watch a lot of TV."

The truth is that Midge deserves recognition. She trained hard and became skilled at going where no big dog can go. With a perfect score she passed the Ohio certification test to become a marijuana-sniffing dog and is in training for state certification in cocaine sniffing.

To my wife and me, though, Midge is also the dog who likes to hide and ambush me when I climb the stairs of our house. She is rambunctious, barking, running, and begging me to get down on the floor and play with her by scratching my pant leg. Each night, after a hard day's work as my partner, she curls up, first on her bed and then on ours. She flips the covers up over her head and has a good night's sleep.

In the morning Midge transforms from a playful two-year-old into a no-nonsense K-9 officer. I outfit her with a black-shirt uniform that has a big, gold sheriff's star on it. Like a horse's harness or a therapy dog's jacket, putting on her uniform is a cue for Midge that it's time for her to go to work. Removing her uniform means she is off duty. Midge's work ethic and uniform help her become very focused. She expects to accompany me every day and gets pretty upset if I don't take her.

On the way to the Geauga County Sheriff's Office, Midge rides in the passenger seat next to me. After we arrive, we walk down the hallway and say good morning to co-workers. Midge pokes her head into their offices, and I can hear them say, "Hi, Midge."

She has her own chair and bed in my office, yet she often sits on my lap while I work. If I leave my desk, she follows me everywhere. Midge works off-lead and hasn't had a leash on her in over a year. Some days we practice training. Other times we respond to calls. We do demonstrations in schools and for community groups. Midge's job is to watch everything I do and always be with me. She even trots along with me to administrative meetings. Midge brings a smile to people's faces and is friendly with everybody. She likes men, women, men with beards, and people wearing sunglasses or coats. Nothing bothers her.

So how did a two-pound, playful puppy become a narcotics dog?

A Big Idea for a Little Dog

The idea of training a smaller dog to sniff out narcotics came while I watched our big German shepherds do searches in confined spaces, such as car interiors. A hundred-pound German shepherd fills up a car's interior or trunk. It's awkward and hard for a dog this size to move. A big dog frequently does damage with his toenails that law enforcement has to pay for if no narcotics are found.

I started thinking that a small dog of about thirty to forty pounds would be able to get into places where the bigger dogs couldn't fit. I looked at animal shelters and rescue places and saw good dogs, but none of them quite clicked with me. Melissa Metz, a woman at work, told me that her parents' two dogs had had a litter, and they had one puppy left. She wondered if I would be interested in seeing the pup.

I asked, "What kind of dog?"

She said, "A Chihuahua."

I just laughed and said, "I don't think so." I didn't want a yippy-yappy dog.

Melissa said that the puppy's mother was a rat terrier. I knew that Jack Russells and rat terriers were hunting-dog breeds. They are very intelligent. Rat terriers were bred to find rats on farms and get rid of vermin hiding onboard sailing vessels.

"How big is the dog?" I asked.

"She's not going to be very big," Melissa said. "She's the runt of the litter."

I wasn't sure about looking at this dog until Melissa came in with pictures of the cute puppy, so I agreed to meet her. When Melissa brought the puppy into our office, the dog was only ten weeks old and weighed two pounds. I could hold her in one hand. But two things impressed me about her. First, she had a very good demeanor and calmness around people. All kinds of strange folks pass through a sheriff's office, so being comfortable and confident would definitely be a plus. Second, I noticed that she sniffed everything. Although only a young puppy, she understood what her nose

Sheriff Dan McClelland's Midge

was for. I decided to give her a chance. I gave her the name Midge, because she reminded me of when our daughter was little and used to play with Barbie dolls. Barbie had a little friend named Midge, and that seemed like a perfect name for our tiny rookie.

K-9 dogs typically belong to the county. Since I was experimenting with Midge because I thought her size would be an advantage in narcotics detection, I thought it better that I adopt her. That way I would not use taxpayer money for an experiment that might not work. Also, if the county owned Midge, she couldn't be given away if things didn't work out. She'd have to be sold at auction, and I didn't want her to go through that.

Training Midge

Midge began training for police work immediately. I talked to the K-9 handlers and trainers at the office. They told me what to do. Their way of training was to teach the dog to work for praise and from loyalty. This meant that Midge and I needed to become best friends and spend time together. Each day when we went to the office, we worked on basic puppy skills, such as housebreaking and obedience commands. We bonded by learning her favorite games and playing. When she was only three and a half months old, we started training for narcotics. This was a remarkably young age, because most German shepherds are eight to ten months old before they start that kind of training. Midge just seemed to be ready for it.

The training is actually quite simple. We use a four-inch-square, one-inch-thick canvas-bag envelope that contains excellent marijuana. The first time I introduced the bag, I played Midge's two favorite games, tug and fetch. I got down on the ground, and we played with the bag. For less than thirty seconds, I let her tug and pull it out of my fingers so that she won. Then I put the bag away. I could see by the look on her face that she thought, "We were playing. I like this. It was fun."

The next day, I took the canvas bag out again. I said, "Get the dope," which would be her cue to do a search. I used only praise and said, "Good girl," when she found the bag. We continued playing fetch and tug for a while, and then I put the bag away. For the second time, she looked as if she wanted to say, "I really liked this. Why did you stop?"

The third day, I opened up the container where I kept the canvas bag and said, "We're going to play." She smelled the marijuana and knew we were going to play. She was ready to go.

The fourth day I had someone hold her in my office. I put the bag behind the door about five to six feet away from her. Then I said, "Get the dope." She immediately retrieved the bag.

To this day, finding narcotics is absolutely a game she plays with me — one in which she gets lots of praise and makes me happy.

Later, our training sessions included my pointing at something, which she'd sniff for me. We had to work with wind and air currents above her head. She needed to ignore distractions, such as other dogs, odors, food, people, and other animals. Her abilities continued to improve.

I had to learn how to read her style of alerting me. I watched her smelling for the narcotics. I noticed that she pushed with her nose, and I could see her nostrils flaring as she sniffed. If it was really quiet, I could hear her sniffing. When she found the dope, she honed in on it. If it was above her head, she stood on back legs, stretched out, and put her nose as close to it as she could. If the object was within her reach on the floor or on a lower shelf, sometimes she'd sniff and scratch.

For safety reasons, I've taught Midge not to retrieve the narcotics. Instead, she stops everything and makes direct eye contact with me in a very obvious gesture, staring for five to ten seconds. She's saying, "I found it. Okay?" At that point I throw a little tennis ball down as a substitute so that she can play with that toy instead of the actual narcotics, which could be dangerous to her. Besides, we don't want her to play with evidence.

If Midge were to sniff narcotics other than marijuana, this could overwhelm her because of her size. In case of an accident, I have an antidote kit with a shot that negates the effects of cocaine. I'd only use this kit as a last resort. It's my job to keep my dog safe. Because she no longer tries to bite or retrieve the package but stops and looks at me, it is a much safer alert signal than if she bit the bag or tried to bring it to me.

Midge's Official Success Stories

Midge has had finds, but we have not yet credited her with an arrest. This is because most of her finds have been in schools. We partner with schools to enforce their zero-tolerance-for-drugs policy. After finding drugs in a student's locker, rather than arresting the student, we're satisfied when a youngster goes into a rehabilitation program and gets counseling to put him or her back on the right track. We would only make an arrest at a school if we found the mother lode in a school locker.

On two occasions Midge has alerted on a residual odor. We didn't find the narcotics in the school lockers, but the students' jackets or sweaters were in the lockers, and Midge detected the odor of drugs on those items. Later the students admitted to having had marijuana in their jacket pockets the day before. If the drug was there, Midge can still smell it.

She has been on narcotics raids and located drugs. However, the bad guys had already been arrested, pursuant to a warrant. Midge just helped us locate additional evidence.

Midge's size is an advantage in confined spaces. I can pick her up and set her in the trunk or interior of a car. A big dog can't do that. We've used Midge in very crowded, small bedrooms. She searches but doesn't knock things over and can go under the bed.

She also searches underneath cars without our having to jack up the car. A drug courier knows the police will look in a glove box, the center console, or other obvious places. Some use secret compartments underneath the car. Midge can go there.

Once a dog starts to pant, his sense of smell diminishes, and he begins using his mouth instead of his nose. Midge doesn't pant easily. This means she can work longer, even in a large room. When we're searching school lockers, she can be the last dog working, because she hasn't started to pant yet.

Midge is a single-purpose dog. She'll never replace the big dog in law enforcement. Big dogs are needed for crowd control and to protect handlers. Midge's single purpose is narcotics detection, and this specialty has obvious value to a police department.

Midge's Unofficial Success Stories

We have received a number of inquiries from law enforcement in other locations. After hearing about Midge, the city of Myrtle Beach put a proposal before their city council to train small dogs for narcotics detection. People from the Office of National Drug Control Policy, out of Washington, D.C., have spoken with me quite a bit about Midge. Some jail administrators have called for consultation, because they were looking for a small dog who could work in cell blocks. Airports and airlines have asked about how Midge works, because a small dog can go inside an airplane and move around in and under the seats.

The military has to deal with explosives. Land mines detonate with twenty-four pounds of compression. Midge only weighs eight pounds. In theory a dog her size could stand on a land mine and not set it off. This would enable K-9s to safely help clear minefields.

All of these developments make me feel excited about and proud of what Midge and I have done.

Midge's uniqueness and pleasant personality have inspired others and me. Youngsters are attracted to her. She loves toddlers. Little children might be scared of a large dog, but they're not afraid of Midge.

I do talks for middle-school students, typically a difficult age bracket to target with a message. Instead of lecturing, I can give a demonstration of Midge's work and weave in messages about the consequences of substance abuse. Because Midge is memorable, students retain the image much better than if I tried to deliver it with words alone.

Usually, in every class I speak to, there are smaller kids, so I incorporate another important message into my presentations. I say, "You don't have to be the biggest one to take a stand. You don't have to be the biggest one to do the right thing. To be somebody, you can be little, and it's fine." Kids really grab onto that idea, and Midge helps them understand it.

Drug Abuse Resistance Education (D.A.R.E.) is a nationwide program aimed at educating fifth and sixth graders about drugs, substance abuse, bullying, violence, and peer pressure. When our county's students graduate from D.A.R.E., they get a T-shirt. I am invited to speak at their graduation, and Midge accompanies me. As part of my talk, I compare the similarities between Midge and the students. They go to school; Midge had to go to school to learn how to do her job. They had to take a test; Midge had to take her certification test. They wear a shirt that says what they stand for; Midge wears a shirt with a badge on it that says what she stands for. Some of them may not be the biggest kids on the block, but neither is Midge. The youngsters are able to see their futures more clearly by looking at Midge and what she has accomplished.

Quite often, I visit special classes and bring Midge. All the youngsters get to hold her, even ones who have motor-skill issues. It's hard for them to hold and pet her, but she's very good with them.

I'm in my thirty-second year in the sheriff's office, and I've only taken one letter home in all those years. It was from the parent of a child with disabilities. Her child was taken out of regular class and put into a special class during the school day, which he hated. The other kids ridiculed and teased him. The letter explained that her child's feelings about being in the special class had changed on the day Midge came to their school. After I let the kids in the special class hold Midge, the boy went back to his regular classroom. By then, word had spread that Midge had visited the special class. All of a sudden the boy wasn't being teased anymore. Instead, he was treated as a hero. The children said, "You got to see Midge, to hold Midge. What's she like?" This one visit turned the youngster's special class into a positive time.

One day, I went to a class for children with learning disabilities and met a young boy who was confined to a wheelchair. An aide stayed with the boy to push buttons on an electronic device on the wheelchair. When this boy saw Midge, the grin on his face spread from ear to ear. I came home that day and told my wife, "I don't care if this dog couldn't find drugs if I tied them to her tail. She makes these children smile."

I believe that Midge sends an important message to youngsters in our town's special-needs classes and to everyone who meets her. She not only holds the record for being the world's smallest K-9 dog, but also she holds a special place in all of our hearts.

MEDITATION

What could you master that you always thought or others have said you were too small to accomplish?

Marvin Paints Pictures of Thankfulness

E. J. Finocchio, DVM
Riverside, Rhode Island

*I*n 2002 I sold my practice and semiretired after thirty-three years as a horse veterinarian. I became the first veterinarian in 135 years to head the Rhode Island SPCA on July 1, 2002. In September 2002 I met the dog who would change the course of my life and transform this animal shelter into a thriving organization with outstanding community-outreach programs.

When I took over the shelter leadership, we were desperate to raise money. Dying and in need of revitalization the year before I came here, the shelter had collected only $9,000 in donations. We are now up to $150,000 in annual donations. Much of this success has been due to Marvin, a black Labrador retriever shelter dog who had three different homes in only a few years, limped on three legs, and managed to steal my heart.

Marvin was brought into the shelter with another dog, named Bear, a large German shepherd mix with whom he had lived. The dogs belonged to a family with a seventeen-year-old girl. They relinquished Marvin and Bear because they didn't have any more time for the dogs in their lives.

Born on the Fourth of July, Marvin had had an injury as a

puppy and couldn't put his right-hind leg on the ground, so he shuffled along on three legs. The family that relinquished Marvin had received him as a Christmas gift puppy on December 24, 1999. Before the family received Marvin, the dog had fallen downstairs in a barn or out of a hayloft. Nobody seemed to know the exact story, only that he had sustained a permanent disability that left him lame.

When people come to an animal shelter, they normally are not interested in adopting a dog with a disability. After his previous family relinquished him, Marvin had been in the kennel for around four to five weeks when a man and his two young children from North Smithfield, Rhode Island, came in. I assured the man that Marvin was a good dog and said, "Marvin gets along very well despite his lameness. It doesn't seem to slow him down."

The reason I could vouch for Marvin was that during the five weeks he had been in the shelter, I visited with him and the other shelter dogs three to four times a week. I brought each a dog biscuit and treats. It is very noisy in the kennels, and all the dogs sought attention by seeing who among them could bark the loudest.

I noticed that Marvin sat in his kennel cage and never barked. Whenever I came by, he pushed his little nose at the screen. I'd offer him a biscuit, which he'd gently take out of my hand. Then we'd look into each other's eyes. When a dog stares at you, it is usually a sign of seeking dominance, but this was different. Marvin held nothing but quiet and gentleness in his gaze.

Marvin went to his new home with the man and his children, but a month later he was back in the shelter. The man said he didn't want to keep an animal with a disability. Our policy is that the people adopting can't sell, trade, or give away the animal. It was very nice of the man to abide by the rules and bring the dog back to us, but now Marvin was here for a second time. He wound up back in the same kennel he had occupied the first time. In another two or three weeks it would be Thanksgiving, but Marvin didn't seem to have a lot of things to be grateful for.

My only son, Tim, was working in Boston. I emailed him that there was a really nice dog here if he or any of his friends might be interested in adopting.

Our next phone conversation went something like this:

"Dad, I live in a condo and work. Why don't you and Mom take Marvin?"

"Your mother would never allow a large, shedding dog in the house. She's an immaculate housekeeper. And besides, she hasn't gotten over being attacked by a dog as a young girl. She's afraid of dogs."

"But, Dad, you need to adopt *this* dog. And you said that Marvin is a nice dog."

I called my wife, Marie, and as I suspected, she gave a definite no to adopting Marvin. She listed her objections: "He sheds. He has a disability. We're not really dog people." In addition to all the reasons she gave, I had to admit we were enjoying freedom from extra responsibilities at home for the first time in years.

Dr. Finocchio's Marvin

I called Tim back and told him about his mother's objections. "Dad," he said, "I still want you to take the dog."

I asked Marie to at least come to the shelter to see Marvin. She agreed to look, and we even played with him. But she was still hesitant about adopting.

I couldn't get over feeling bad for Marvin. Whenever he looked into my eyes, there was such a strong connection. I told my staff that instead of keeping Marvin in the kennel, they should bring him to our front office so that he could socialize with Linda, the receptionist.

I happened to be there when Linda put Marvin in her office. Although he never barked in the kennels, in Linda's office the dog wouldn't stop howling. Linda said, "It won't work."

When I entered the reception room, Marvin looked at me and stopped barking, so I decided to let him come to my office. He crawled under my huge oak desk and lay there. If I stood up to go someplace, he followed me wherever I went. It seemed that I had acquired a furry black shadow.

The first day Marvin stayed in my office, at five o'clock, it was time to go home, but I didn't have the heart to put this dog back in the kennels. I asked Linda to get a big crate and keep him in the foyer overnight. She was concerned that, by eight in the morning when I returned, he might have messed in his crate. I said, "Let's try it for two or three nights."

Marvin never made a mess. The next day, he again followed me all around the shelter.

Thanksgiving was coming, and Tim continued to nag me. My son would call and say, "Are you taking the dog home?"

"Tim, there are sixteen people coming to our house for Thanksgiving dinner tomorrow. It would be traumatic for the dog."

"I want you to bring the dog home, Dad."

Because Tim is our only child, he rules our life, but I stuck to my plan and didn't take the dog home on Thanksgiving Eve.

On Thanksgiving Day, Tim said, "You're going to go get Marvin."

Our guests were to arrive at one o'clock in the afternoon. I headed to the shelter around ten in the morning to pick up Marvin. That was five years ago. He has been coming home with me ever since. Marvin is now my wife's best friend and a big part of all my family. I guess this is because he chose me.

Marvin Becomes an Artist

I read an article about elephants wrapping their trunks around brushes and doing paintings. People were paying large amounts of money to buy them. The journalist noted that the elephants showed artistic talent, because the paintings were more than linear and vertical strokes.

Marvin wags his tail so much that I wondered, "What if I put paint on his tail and held some paper underneath it?"

One day, I randomly placed nontoxic watercolor paint on Marvin's tail, held his canvas, and let Marvin wag his tail onto it. Although the colors smeared together, I thought, "Wow, this is so impressionistic." It actually looked nice.

So I announced to Tim and Marie that I was going to have Marvin paint. They snickered. I went to our finished basement and did some paintings with Marvin. I brought the paintings upstairs and asked what they thought.

They said the paintings were not bad.

I asked, "What do you think we should do? It will cost about $5 or $6 to frame them."

They started getting excited, and Marie said, "You could sell the paintings for $10 or $15."

"What, are you crazy? That's ridiculous," I stated. "We can sell these paintings for more than that."

Tim said, "Those paintings will never sell for more than $15."

Marvin has been painting for four years now. One of his paintings sold for $2,500. We sell his prints for $50.

Marvin's paintings are unbelievable. Some look like actual figures of flowers, birds, and animals. If you ask ten people what they see in one of Marvin's paintings of a rose, ten people say they see a rose. If he's painted a butterfly, everyone will see a butterfly. There is no question what you are looking at, even though he paints with his tail and appears to be hitting the canvas randomly.

People have written articles about Marvin's artistic talents, and he has been on radio and television, but we do not pay to promote his artwork. His MarvArt has been exhibited at the Scituate Art Festival, one of the top three art festivals in Rhode Island, and at the Burrillville Arts and Crafts Festival. Maxwell Maze, a nationally famous artist from Rhode Island, invited Marvin to exhibit his paintings with prominent Rhode Island artists for the Audubon Society's 2005 Fur, Fin, and Feathers Art Show. Marvin's paintings are always on display at the Rhode Island SPCA.

With earnings from Marvin's paintings and the children's book I wrote about him, *Marvelous Marvin*, the Marvin Fund was created at the Rhode Island SPCA, a private nonprofit humane society. To date, the fund has raised over $85,000. All the proceeds in the Marvin Fund help defray the cost of medical expenses for pets who need surgery and outfit them with carts or other devices so they can live as normal a life as possible. Another way we use the Marvin Fund is to allow the elderly and people with disabilities to keep their pets. These pets are often best friends for the elderly, the sick, or people with disabilities. If people have to give up their dogs or cats due to illness or inability to pay for veterinary care, it is devastating to them. Marvin makes sure that doesn't happen.

Marvin's Children's Book

Marie and I adopted Marvin in November 2002. In only five months, I had finished writing a book about him and published it in March 2003.

In the book, I included the little we knew of Marvin's past. He was born the runt in a litter of nine puppies in Maryland. He was the Christmas present for a teenage Rhode Island girl. She loved Marvin and cried when her family gave the dog to our shelter. Over the years, she sometimes visited him and always shed tears when she saw and had to part with him again.

I wrote the first draft of the book in two nights, with Marvin sitting at my feet. I believed that people had to read his story. Before it was published, everyone I asked to read it cried. For a book to evoke such deep emotions, I knew it must be a worthwhile project. I thought we could sell the book and raise money to support the work of the Rhode Island SPCA and the Marvin Fund.

We initially printed a thousand copies and did no advertising except for putting up a poster at the shelter. The book has a yellow cover with a picture of Marvin and is titled *Marvelous Marvin*. There is no subtitle, but the poster for it has a line of text that says, "The story about a dog who was given a second chance."

Marvelous Marvin has helped make him the poster dog in Rhode Island, an example of an animal you can get in a shelter. You don't have to go to a fancy breeder. And you certainly don't need to support places that sell dogs from puppy mills.

The reason I never forget where Marvin comes from is the collar he wears. It is from a black Lab who was put to sleep because no one wanted to give him a home. I took the collar off the black Lab after I humanely put him to rest. Then I placed it on Marvin as a reminder of what could have been his fate and in respect for other unwanted animals in shelters all over the world. Marvin will always wear that collar.

People started buying Marvin's book. Teachers began reading it to their classes and invited Marvin to school for Reading Week. We have now sold over three thousand books.

Marvin Helps the Children

Marvin is very sensitive. He has an affinity for children that is hard to explain. There are pictures on Marvin's website of him with young schoolchildren and toddlers.

I take Marvin to schools, where he teaches children not to go with strangers or accept anything from people they don't know. The children gather around Marvin and me. We have Marvin sit in front of them, and I ask the children to call him.

They say, "Here, Marvin." He will not move.

I put some biscuits under his nose and on his paw. I tell the kids to say, "Marvin, eat your biscuit." He will not eat it.

Then I say, "You can go, Marvin," and unlike when the children called him, he comes to me. I tell him to eat a biscuit, and although he wouldn't eat it when the children gave it to him, he will eat it for me.

This demonstration hopefully gets the point across that children should follow Marvin's example and not listen to strangers or go with people they don't know.

I tell the kids that this is a fun day and that we will pick one of them to go with Marvin and me to spend a day at the park, just the three of us. It is surprising how many children would go with me, a stranger, on the spur of the moment. They get excited about being with the dog and let their guard down. With Marvin's demonstration, we show how important it is for them to never, ever go with a stranger unless their parents give them permission, to never take anything from a stranger unless their parents say they can have it.

If we save one child's life, we will have accomplished our goal. The teachers tell me that our Strangers Are Danger program is very meaningful to the children. I continue to be amazed at what one dog can accomplish.

Marvin's Community Service

Marvin's therapy-dog work began shortly after we adopted him. I began to experience close-up what a calm, yet friendly, dog he is. On the thirty-five-minute commute from our home to the animal shelter, Marvin lies on the front seat with his head resting on my lap. Nothing fazes him. He doesn't look out the car window as other dogs would. I always feel that it's good therapy for me to pet and touch his soft ears. I talk to him on these commutes, but he never answers me back, verbally that is.

At the shelter Marvin has the freedom to roam around as he

pleases, but he never leaves my side. He greets every person who comes into the shelter. If they want him to, he licks their faces. He lies down to let people caress and pet him, but mostly, he waits for them to supply him with treats.

A person can be black, yellow, green, pink, tall, fat, skinny, short, disabled, uniformed, or nonuniformed, and Marvin accepts the person for what he or she is on the inside. The mailman is his best friend. Marvin gets the mail from him and brings it in to us.

I was a horse veterinarian all my life, so I had never heard of the Delta Society or pet therapy. I did not train Marvin to be a certified therapy dog. I never had time to do any of that, because my job is so hectic.

The March after we adopted Marvin, when we'd only had him for five months, I heard that the Delta Society was evaluating potential therapy dogs at a kennel in Exeter, Rhode Island. It was on a Saturday, so on a lark, I brought Marvin to be evaluated. The people running the program said to bring his brush and lead.

Marvin made the highest score of the thirteen dogs who were evaluated that day. He was awarded the Delta Society's Pet Partners certificate on the spot.

Since then, Marvin and I have visited over a hundred different facilities, including hospitals, nursing homes, rehabilitation centers, day care centers, schools, libraries, and summer camps. We went to Paul Newman's Hole in the Wall Gang Camp in Connecticut and met children who are HIV-positive or have sickle-cell anemia. We visit Hasbro Children's Hospital in Rhode Island once a month. The people at the hospital say that Marvin is mind-bogglingly well behaved.

Although it came about by chance, Marvin is an absolutely great therapy dog.

Marvin and I regularly go to nursing homes. Usually the patients gather around us with me in the middle and Marvin lying on the rug while I talk with the people. Some of the elderly comprehend what I'm saying and some don't. But Marvin evokes times from their pasts when they had dogs. Many of them truly enjoy his visits.

We have been to twenty or thirty nursing homes, and Marvin never barks unless I ask him to. Marvin makes his rounds and lets residents pet him and give him biscuits. He is never animated. But one day he surprised me by going over to an elderly lady who was sitting in a chair and starting to bark at her. I was embarrassed, because this was abnormal behavior for Marvin. When we're in these homes, sometimes people doze off, and I hoped he hadn't frightened the woman. It turned out that she had fainted and Marvin had picked up on it. The nurses immediately tended to her. We couldn't explain how he knew that lady had fainted, but he sensed something unusual and barked to get help.

In a personal meeting with Rhode Island Governor Donald Carcieri (the owner of one of Marvin's paintings), Marvin received a citation. In 2007 the Rhode Island House of Representatives passed a resolution honoring Marvin for his community service. The Marvin Fund received $12,000 from a prestigious state organization. He has met two city mayors. Much of my day revolves around Marvin's schedule of visitations and events. I have to keep a special log for Marvin's appointments. Rhode Island is a small state, so there is a large percentage of the population that knows who Marvin is. He could run for office on his name recognition.

What Marvin Has Taught Me

Dogs tend to become angry and introverted if they are abandoned. They get cage rage and are not happy campers in the kennels. Marvin was sent to the shelter twice, through no fault of his own, and you'd think he'd be bitter. But he put the past with its loneliness and homelessness behind him and moved on with his life. He ignores his disability. He seems very appreciative of what has happened to him and doesn't dwell on the negatives, if such traits are possible for a dog.

I truly believe Marvin enjoys what he's doing. If he did not like it, he would balk or hesitate, but he's always ready to go to a school and see the kids. Marie puts an appropriate kerchief on him before he leaves for work with me and takes it off every night when we come home. My wife matches my neckties with Marvin's kerchiefs, and the dog wears a different one every single day. Some of the kids make kerchiefs for Marvin with his name on them.

One or more individuals each day come to our shelter to visit Marvin or bring their children. At one hundred years old, Mrs. Feole was our oldest visitor to the shelter. Her daughter brought her to meet Marvin, and we have a photograph of her visit on Marvin's website.

Marvin and I help the elderly, disabled, and mentally and physically challenged. These are not people who send thank-you cards or donations. The wealth of giving is our greatest reward. A pat on the back would actually distract from the feeling of serving people who do not have anything.

Even though I am in my sixties, I learned much about life on the other side of the tracks because of Marvin. I'm thankful for what

I have and all that Marvin has exposed me to. I would never have gone to see young children with IVs in their arms getting therapy. I would never have seen the faces of elderly people whose children have forgotten them in nursing homes. I would never have brought cheer to the homeless. Marvin has shown me a completely different side of life.

Marvin also shows me how to find joy in simple things. To go outside, chase a ball, roll in the grass, and just hang out with him is peaceful and calming. The world goes by so rapidly that most of us don't have time to sit by a stream, throw a ball, watch the clouds go by, or see the sun shining over a meadow. I'm a pragmatic person, but these are some of the things this dog has taught me that have enriched my life.

Marvin is eight years old now, with gray starting to appear under his chin. He has had a mission to help those who cannot help themselves, encourage people to never give up hope, and give animals in need a second chance. Both of us will continue to inspire and help others by spreading joy, happiness, and hope. Marvin never gave up and cherishes his second chance.

MEDITATION

Has an animal enabled you to have a second chance at life in ways you never expected?

At-Risk Teens Train At-Risk Dogs

Lisa LaVerdiere
Stillwater, Minnesota

At Home for Life, the sanctuary in Star Prairie, Wisconsin, that I founded in 1997, I got a call one day from a young girl who lived in a tough neighborhood on the east side of St. Paul. She said that her family's dog, Emily, had had puppies, and some men took them to use as bait for pit-bull fighting. While Emily fought to save her puppies, the men kicked her, breaking her leg. Emily had been nursing her pups when the men stole them, so she still had all her milk.

The girl who called us got a ride and left Emily at our veterinarian's office. On our forty acres on the Apple River, we provide a home for rescued animals from all over the United States and Canada who are not able to find adoptive homes due to old age, disabilities, and medical and behavioral issues. We decided to bring Emily to Home for Life and give her a new chance at happiness.

When I picked up Emily at Dr. Bailey's office, I saw that she was a bassadore, a dog with the short legs and long body of a basset hound mixed with the short, black coat of a Labrador retriever. Emily had not had any veterinary care for her injuries, so Dr. Bailey treated her for the broken leg. She would be in a cast for two months.

After I brought her to the sanctuary, Emily cried constantly for a while. But I found it amazing that the moment I decided Emily would stay with us permanently, she immediately relaxed and no longer whined or appeared nervous. She seemed to understand the meaning of the words *Home for Life*.

It was a joy to watch Emily become more confident, secure, and happy. She quickly made new dog friends, and her BFF (best friend forever) is Sabra, a young Afghan. Emily shows leadership qualities and is heir apparent to Foxy, who is alpha dog in her group.

Since Emily was young and loving, we put her in the Renaissance Project at Boys Totem Town.

The Renaissance Project and Boys Totem Town

The Renaissance Project began in 1998 when Janet Tomlinson, a high-school teacher at the Renaissance High School in River Falls, Wisconsin, and I got the idea to have students from alternative high schools train Home for Life dogs for certification as therapy dogs and serve in our community-outreach projects.

After Janet retired from teaching at the high school, I proposed to Tom McGinn, superintendent at Boys Totem Town in St. Paul, Minnesota, to run the Renaissance Project as a pilot project with their adolescents. Tom thought it would be a great partnership.

Boys Totem Town is licensed to provide six to ten months of highly structured yet nurturing treatment and three months of aftercare for boys adjudicated as delinquents by the juvenile court. In this juvenile corrections facility, since they must do extra programs for school credit, these troubled teens could train our dogs. Many of the teens had been involved in dog fighting. They came from a tough culture. We would show them a different way of relating to dogs.

Emily and Daryl Make a Perfect Match

We began the first session at Boys Totem Town in winter 2007. I chose Daryl (not his real name), a seventeen-year-old boy, to work with Emily. I paired up dogs and trainers according to the similarities in their personalities, temperaments, and physical traits, such as how athletic they were and the way they communicated through body language. Emily is long, round, and short with shiny, black fur.

Daryl is a stocky black kid. I assumed that Daryl, like Emily, must have gone through rough times.

Although Daryl and Emily turned out to be a great match, initially he was upset about the assignment. All the boys wanted to work with the macho, big dogs, not the smaller ones. But, to me, Daryl and Emily looked as if they were born to be together.

Lisa's Emily and Daryl

I told Tom that I didn't want to be briefed about the teens' backgrounds. That worked well, because the boys knew that I didn't know anything about them. This kept me from judging them or being shocked and choked up at finding out what they had done. I believe that we all have both good and bad inside of us, so I was willing to let the boys start my program with a clean slate. The youngsters who come to Boys Totem Town have lived in environments where they had no support or nurturing. Until now, nobody motivated them to get to work or go to school.

The Initial Training

I was supernervous the first few class sessions of the initial training, but it was great to see the teens starting to have fun with the dogs. Daryl and nine other boys worked one-on-one with Emily and the other dogs twice a week in the gym at Boys Totem Town.

In an effort to show the teens what careers were available for working with dogs and other animals, on Wednesdays each week, the boys and dogs went to the University of Minnesota's Veterinarian School and visited the dog hydrotherapy program. We also took the boys to see the St. Paul Police Department give demonstrations with their K-9 dogs. Tom told me that he liked my vocational view of the program. The boys could discover possible future jobs with dogs, such as groomer or veterinary assistant. By taking them to see the K-9 dogs, they could connect with police in a whole new way.

Each dog had a boy's individual attention, and the dogs got out of the sanctuary for exposure to a lot of new places. We brought the dogs to various crowds, around schools, and into offices. The dogs learned to be comfortable with all kinds of strangers and situations. Students and administrators posed as patients in hospitals or as doctors. By teaching high-level obedience skills, the dogs would be able to pass the Therapy Dogs International and AKC (American Kennel Club) Canine Good Citizen tests. This would make them eligible to participate in our Home for Life programs and visit hospitals, nursing homes, and mental health care facilities.

I took the teens on field trips to see our community outreach in action. I felt that it was important for Daryl and the other boys to learn that Emily and the other dogs in training would have their lives enhanced because they knew how to behave. One highlight for the teens was when they learned that their dogs would bring comfort in domestic-abuse shelters. This was very meaningful for many of the boys, since they had lived at shelters before, as little children fleeing violence.

Giving Daryl and Emily a Chance to Shine

At first, Daryl and the other boys tended to have defeatist attitudes. A lot of them asked, "What if I fail or don't get through the test?" Over the course of the program, Daryl and Emily bonded. I watched as he took pride in training her.

One of the things I taught the teens was that thoughts are things and they can learn to control their thoughts. Working with the dogs helped them experience the power of images. The dogs were barometers for how the boys were thinking. As trainers they had to learn to be calm, assertive, positive, and patient. I advised them to always keep in their minds a strong image of the dog being successful. I said, "The dogs will get you there."

In the beginning, I had to hold a high degree of confidence for all of the boys. They grew more self-assured as the program continued. Most had never had even one success or achieved anything in their lives. I encouraged the teens by talking about their strengths and not dwelling on their shortcomings. They had a view of themselves as losers or not as good as everybody else.

The social workers, psychiatrists, and teachers at Boys Totem Town are specially trained to work with the boys' emotions and backgrounds. I didn't delve into their issues because I believed it was outside my boundaries. Our program was supposed to be fun, even though training dogs is hard work. The boys didn't want to talk about their problems, and I didn't ask them to confide in me, although I stayed open to listening to them. I began to notice how eager these boys were to work with the dogs. They wore their Home for Life rubber bracelets all over the school.

I always kept our sessions positive. During the training we played rock music such as the Monkees and rap music without violent lyrics. The music created an atmosphere of fun for the kids and dogs. It helped the dogs learn to work in a noisy environment. The nursing homes and hospitals they would visit someday as therapy dogs could be chaotic at times.

It was a special day when Emily passed all the tests to become a certified therapy dog. She would soon visit children at a pediatric oncology ward. At the end of the training program, I wrote Daryl and each of the other boys a thank-you note about how great they were and what an achievement they had accomplished. They received certificates when they finished. I like to think this program is something they will always remember with pride.

Daryl and Emily Meet Cesar Millan

In 2007 Home for Life had a big fundraising event with Cesar Millan, star of the National Geographic Channel's series *Dog Whisperer*, as our guest of honor. Tom let the boys view Cesar's DVDs before meeting him. Tom said the kids were thrilled to see Cesar in action.

Daryl and another boy, both graduates from the first dog-training class, wanted to meet Cesar. They were to give a private demonstration of how they trained the Renaissance Project dogs. By this time the two youngsters no longer lived at Boys Totem Town but were supposed to catch a bus there to get to their meeting with Cesar. They never showed up. Maybe they were scared or had an upset with family members. They might have lost confidence in themselves to demonstrate in front of such a big celebrity.

However, at the fundraising gala, Daryl and the other boys did meet Cesar and even posed for pictures with him. We had arranged for a volunteer barber to cut the boys' hair and had them all dressed up. It was thrilling to watch Daryl and Emily, and the other boys parade with their dogs around the hall for the cheering crowd of three hundred donors.

What's Next?

Tom and I don't have data yet to prove the positive outcomes we observed. The boys and dogs both seemed to flourish though. Tom said, "The kids from the first program became calmer and more responsible and respectful. I can see that, by having the boys teach social skills to the dogs, their understanding and trust grew."

Being in the Renaissance Project helped our dogs too. They looked forward to the time spent with their trainers. Dogs are very schedule oriented, and they knew exactly when they were supposed to go to class. They were excited and anticipated working with the boys. Dogs love to learn. Their brains need to be engaged, and with the Renaissance Project we found a great way to take care of the dogs' minds as well as their bodies and emotions.

Tom said that Daryl has returned to the community, and from all accounts so far, things are going well for him. Daryl works at a job, and goes to school and church. He also participates in a basketball program. "The first year is the toughest one," Tom told me. "There are no reports of Daryl's being involved in gang activities, and he's tested negative on drugs."

Time will tell everything that Home for Life dogs such as Emily can do for at-risk youths like Daryl. The dogs needed their minds stimulated and their hearts opened to trust humans again. The boys needed to learn responsibility and to love and be loved by a dog. It looks as if the Renaissance Project at Boys Totem Town is meeting both of these goals.

MEDITATION

How have dogs transformed your life when you felt most vulnerable or at risk?

Whispering Secrets to Anna at Ground Zero

Sarah R. Atlas
Barrington, New Jersey

*N*o billboards advertise, "Here's how to get involved in search-and-rescue work." Yet I had wanted for a long time to give this type of service. I remember watching a television program in which search-and-rescue dogs responded to an earthquake in a far-off land. The handlers and dogs worked under the worst conditions to assist those in life-and-death situations. I wondered whether I ever would be in the right circumstances to find the best dog to fulfill my dream.

I had been involved with my older dog in *schutzhund*, a sport that originated in Germany for demonstrating a dog's intelligence and courage. It involves competing in a dog triathlon that includes obedience training, tracking, and protection work. So I had some idea of the time and energy commitment required to train a dog to a high level of ability. I decided to add a puppy to my household of two dogs. In February 1998 I went to look at a litter of German shepherd puppies from imported bloodlines. As I pondered which to choose, a little bicolored pup marched over, grabbed my pants leg, and tugged on it. I said, "I guess I've been picked." Her name was Anna. With that first connection, we would begin the journey of a lifetime.

I'd had quite a few dogs over the years, but right away I could tell that Anna was different from all the rest. She seemed to know what I was thinking before I asked her to do things. Also, she was very protective. Anna and I were in tune and so connected with each other that, even when separated physically, I felt her presence with me. This was a unique spiritual experience for me to have with a dog.

While at my job one day, I happened to have a conversation with a married couple, Sharon and Rich. They were both emergency medical technicians (EMTs) and were also involved in search-and-rescue work with their dogs. I told them about my puppy, Anna, and that she would be perfect in this type of job. They rolled their eyes, because everyone thinks he or she has a perfect dog. "Maybe your dog can find you," Sharon said, "but search-and-rescue dogs must look for strangers."

Rich and Sharon invited me to come to their house so they could evaluate my dog to see if she would be suitable for search-and-rescue training. An important trait for the dog to have is a hunting drive. They repeatedly threw balls into the woods to see if Anna would keep focused on hunting for and finding them. They also had me take Anna away after they threw a ball and return with her five minutes later to see if she continued to look for the ball. To my delight Anna tested extremely well.

Sharon and Rich spent hundreds of hours teaching Anna and me the skills we would need to become a search-and-rescue dog team. One day Rich told me that New Jersey Task Force One, the state's urban search-and-rescue team, was holding a screening for dogs and handlers to become new members. There are only twelve positions on a search-and-rescue team, so only the most talented dogs are selected to join.

Anna was six weeks pregnant when I took her through the screening process. Not only did we make it onto the team's roster, but we also passed with high marks. Soon afterward, Anna had her litter. A year later, we were called to serve at the World Trade Center on September 11, 2001.

Anna at the World Trade Center

Within hours after the airplanes had crashed into the Twin Towers, Anna and I were part of the first search-and-rescue teams arriving at the World Trade Center. As we entered the search area, all that was left of the magnificent Twin Towers were mounds of twisted steel, cables, and white ash, which covered everything. At one point we were halted in our progress with the search as World Trade Center building 7 collapsed onto the pile of debris.

It was frightening with so much commotion. Normally dogs become very intense and excited as they pull ahead to begin their searches. But Anna remained quiet, even stoic, as she looked at the horrible scene in front of us. I confided to Anna that I was scared. I stressed to her that what we were about to do here was important work. She leaned against me as if she understood the gravity of the situation.

This was Anna's first mission. Although we had been through a lot of training, no amount could have prepared us for the sight that lay before us. Everybody looked like little ants against rubble piles of steel and pulverized concrete.

It was so tough. A lot of firemen and cops bent down and cried, whispering into Anna's ears that day. Anna licked the faces of people as she listened to their sorrows and kept their secrets.

Working at Ground Zero was bizarre and eerie. Something very strange happened down there that I have not told many people. Although there were no signs of life, I could hear high-pitched cries and moaning. I saw what looked like white clouds going to heaven. I thought that the moans I heard must have been final cries of spirits leaving their bodies though they did not want to go. Yet they were finally being released. Later on, a fireman who had also worked at Ground Zero said he experienced exactly the same things.

Sarah and Anna

At night we stayed in the Javits Center parking garage, sleeping on blankets on the floor. That first night, Anna and I were exhausted, and I reached over to hug her. She leaned on me and whimpered as we comforted each other.

On the last shift we worked at Ground Zero, a fire chief came up to me and said, "I know remains are up there, but we don't know where to begin searching." So I sent Anna to search in places where none of us could climb. I had to use voice and hand signals to direct her. She showed interest in two spots. She wasn't certified as a cadaver dog, but as closely as we had worked with our search-and-rescue dogs, we understood their body language. Anna stared back at me with intensity until I acknowledged that she must have picked up the scent of remains. Then she walked back down from the area, and I pointed out the locations to the fire chief.

By this time Anna's tongue was turning purple, her breathing was labored, and her eyes looked listless. She was showing signs of heat stroke. I called my task force leader and said that my dog needed medical attention and IV fluids. As I walked back to the vehicle for Anna, a man held up a picture and thrust it toward me. He said, "Please, have you seen my son? Don't leave my son. He's down there somewhere."

I tried to explain to the distraught man that my dog was exhausted, and other dogs were coming. The heat was unbearable from fires still burning. The man pulled something out of a brown paper bag and showed it to me. "This is my son's shirt," he said. I got emotional and had to turn away. Our task force leader explained to the man that rested search dogs were en route to the site.

After I made it to the search-and-rescue vehicle, I heard a call on the radio. A voice confirmed that the searchers had located the remains of two victims in Anna's search area.

After September 11

Following our service on September 11, we packed our belongings and said good-bye to fellow rescuers, well-wishers, and janitorial staff who had become like family. We thanked the police officers who guarded us and the Salvation Army volunteers who fed and consoled us. Then we boarded busses with our tired dogs, their coats thick with soot and an awful smell that would be almost impossible to remove. As our bus pulled out of the Javits Center garage and headed down the West Side Highway, we passed people who began to cheer and shout, "Thank you. Thank you. You are our heroes."

Upon returning to our home base at the Lakehurst Naval Air

Engineering Station, we were greeted by scores of television reporters who pushed microphones toward our faces. Families rushed to hug us. The U.S. Navy band played, and the New Jersey State Police performed "Amazing Grace" on their bagpipes. But, like my fellow teammates, I was very tired and all my muscles were so sore. I was not feeling well.

Anna was not well either. She lay listlessly on the floor, refusing to eat or play. I grew increasingly worried about her. I work for Virtua Health in New Jersey, which had numerous paramedics on the Ground Zero site. Our employer gave us a mandatory week off. After I rested, I returned and worked two shifts as an EMT, responding to 911 calls for medical emergencies, but became very ill and had to be rushed to the hospital. Having problems breathing, I was admitted to the pulmonary care unit with my lung close to collapse and in severe respiratory distress.

Because I needed to spend a week in the hospital, I was distraught without my Anna. The nurses reminded me that dogs were not allowed in the hospital. "I want my dog. She was my partner at 9/11," I said. Later I read in their notes that they thought I was obsessing over Anna. No one understood that she had become part of my soul.

When the administrators learned of the ordeals Anna and I had shared, they made arrangements for her to come to the hospital. On the day of her visit, Anna got off the elevator and sniffed. Then she pulled away from my friend who had brought her to me and bounded into my room. Anna jumped onto my hospital bed. We were so relieved to see each other again that I cried and she whined. Anna could not get close enough. It was as though she tried to crawl into my skin. She stayed in bed with me until visiting hours were over. It was so hard when she had to leave.

I came home to find Anna in even worse shape than she had been before I was hospitalized. The slightest attempt to pet her made her scream with pain. I took Anna for acupuncture and chiropractic treatments, and gave her muscle relaxants to ease her pain. My veterinarian did spinal X-rays and blood work. They revealed that Anna had holes in the discs of her vertebrae.

Going through 9/11 together was an emotional experience that Anna and I had shared. I got my strength from her and from God. There was no way I would refuse to do anything that might help her recover, even though my means were limited.

Due to illness from my service at Ground Zero, I wound up being out of work for two months. During that time the University of Pennsylvania School of Veterinary Medicine received a grant to study the effects of toxins on the dogs who worked at the World Trade Center and the Pentagon. I enrolled Anna in this study, since her medicine alone cost $500 a month. Between my employer and the clinical staff at the university, Anna's entire medical bills were covered. They added up to more than I had paid for my house.

The veterinarians' diagnosis was that Anna had contracted a bacterial and fungal infection in her major organs, along with bone deterioration of the discs in her vertebrae. They told me that my dog would not be able to work any longer.

When the media learned about Anna's illness, her story made national headlines. The outpouring of sympathy and support were tremendous. Get-well cards, faxes, flowers, and dog toys poured in from all over the country. Many cards were simply addressed to

"Search Dog Anna, Barrington, New Jersey." I received emails from as far away as Israel. Telling Anna's story became a healing tool for me, even though I had not sought this kind of attention.

Saying Good-bye to Anna

On August 1, 2002, Anna could no longer lift her head. I rushed to the University of Pennsylvania's Matthew J. Ryan Veterinary Hospital with the sad knowledge that Anna would not come home with me. As we drove, I quietly spoke to her. She laid her head on my lap while I cried. My older shepherd, Josie, acted like Anna's big sister and accompanied me that day.

At the hospital her veterinarian, Dr. Cynthia Otto, rushed Anna to the emergency room. The next day, the awful phone call came. I hurried with Josie to the hospital to see Anna again as she lay on the steel gurney that Dr. Otto had wheeled into a quiet room.

I called Anna's name. Recognizing my voice, she valiantly tried to hold up her head. Anna was placed on the floor with blankets underneath her for comfort and warmth. Josie needed to say good-bye to Anna too. She gingerly walked up to Anna, sniffing her body from head to toe. Gently she licked Anna's face one last time. Then she left the room and lay down in the hallway, her grief clearly visible with the look of sadness in her eyes.

Veterinarians, lab technicians, and hospital staff members arrived in the room to see Anna. I thanked Anna for all the work she had done to bring closure to families of victims of the World Trade Center and tearfully said good-bye to her.

Anna's loss was devastating not only to me but also to everyone who knew of her wonderful contributions. She became the only dog in history to have an obituary in *USA Today*. Anna also inspired a local senior citizen to create a quilt in her honor that traveled internationally in tribute to Anna and all the search dogs who worked tirelessly in those awful days and weeks. In 2003 the Humane Society of the United States posthumously presented Anna with a Genesis Award for the service she gave after the World Trade Center attacks on 9/11.

I still believe that Anna became gravely ill as a result of the service she so selflessly gave. Health studies on the dogs made national headlines concluding that none of the dogs' illnesses and deaths could be attributed to the time they had spent at Ground Zero or the Pentagon. Some of the handlers whose dogs were healthy despite their 9/11 service did not agree with the opinions that I continued to express about the cause of Anna's death.

One night I was sleeping in my bed, and I smelled Anna's distinctive scent. She had always snuggled tightly against me while we slept. I woke up and said, "Good girl, Anna." Of course, she was not actually there, but spiritually she remained with me.

Anna's Successor

Before my current job with Virtua Health, I held a part-time job as an EMT with the Haddonfield, New Jersey, fire department. Anna would accompany me to work. Local elementary-school children would stop by the fire department to give Anna a pat or a cookie and hopefully receive a lick from her in return. The parents would tell their children to let Anna sniff them so that, if they ever were lost, my dog could find them.

As news spread about the terrorist attacks and the lives lost, parents called the schools in Haddonfield asking how to deal with their children, who were upset and crying. It seems that with news coverage continuing twenty-four hours a day, the children feared that thousands of people could not find their way home.

When the newspapers announced that Anna was sick and could no longer perform her search work, the Haddonfield children once again became upset. Without Anna, who would find them if they got lost?

Pam Probst, a teacher at one of Haddonfield's three elementary schools, talked with her fellow educators about how to turn the children's fear into motivation toward positive action. They decided to show that kids can make a difference. The children would hold a walkathon and raise the funds necessary for me to purchase a new search and rescue partner.

On a sunny winter day, seven hundred elementary-school children walked, sang, and skipped around the high-school track. Pam Probst oversaw the collection of donated money. Any money that wasn't used for my new dog went into an emergency fund for supporting search-and-rescue dogs. This program brought our community together in wonderful ways.

It took nine months for me to find the right dog, another German shepherd, named Tango. This dark-sable male from the Netherlands had a magnificent, huge, boxy head. I often think that Anna had a hand in helping me locate her replacement, but she never got to meet Tango.

On the day Tango arrived, I had mixed feelings due to missing Anna, the dog who had been my beloved partner and friend for four years. The kids at the school again rallied to comfort me. They had a welcoming reception for my new dog and held up signs that read, "Tango rocks. We love you, Tango." He returned their affection by rolling over for a belly rub when the children gathered around to meet him. This made me laugh. It was the start of my healing journey with a comical dog who could bring joy to my life once again.

Anna Remembered

A little over a year after Anna's death, I was invited to Camden, New Jersey, to take part in a fireman's muster in which old and antique firefighting apparatuses were on display. I was asked to set up a display there about search-and-rescue dogs.

While I was there, a fireman came up to talk to me. He said, "Sarah Atlas, I have been looking for you. I'm the fire chief who asked you to locate remains. Your dog found the remains of our two firemen. I want to thank you. Their remains were under one of the stairwells. They were both firefighters, and finding them made me feel better, because it brought closure." The entire area had been a jungle of wire, rebar, and steel beams. None of us could discern anything in it. But Anna had found the two firemen, and this made me very satisfied. Anna and all the dogs had done a phenomenal job.

On the sixth anniversary of 9/11, I was invited to read names of the deceased. Since Anna and I had been part of one of the first search-and-rescue dog teams to work at the World Trade Center, my search-and-rescue dog, Tango, and I were to represent the dogs who had worked there. It was an honor to go back to the anniversary memorial. After my reading, a fire chief stopped me and said, "Your dogs took very big hits to help us locate our brothers. We appreciate the job you did. I am sorry your dogs are dying."

Anna's Legacy

In 2005 Anna's courage and compassion inspired me to found the Search and Rescue Dog Foundation. This is a nonprofit organization to assist volunteer K-9 handlers when they must replace dogs who can no longer do search work.

What most people don't realize is that it's volunteers who man search-and-rescue teams. Police dogs, narcotics detection dogs, and fire department arson-detection dogs are all provided for with tax dollars. Yet search-and-rescue dog handlers pay all their own expenses for putting the dogs into service, including vehicle maintenance, travel costs, training, upkeep, veterinarian bills, and dog food.

It is an honor to serve after an emergency or disaster, but it takes two to three years to get an urban search-and-rescue dog certified at a $10,000 cost. Sometimes we start with puppies, only to learn that they might be afraid to climb ladders or have health issues. Then we have to begin all over again with a new dog.

Tango was a young adult who had obedience training and showed potential. This meant that he was much more costly, because someone had already invested a year's worth of work in him. I could not have gotten him without the kindness of other people, most of whom I had never met. I wanted to repay everybody. I wanted to help other handlers.

In 2007, for the first time, my foundation was able to give two $500 grants to assist search-and-rescue dog handlers whose dogs were unable to work or had died due to age, illness, or injury. Our goal is to give ten $1,000 grants per year to help handlers replace K-9s.

Not a day goes by without my thinking of Anna. I began the

Search and Rescue Dog Foundation in her honor, to help my fellow volunteer search-and-rescue workers and to encourage young people to perform this type of service. I think Anna would have liked that.

MEDITATION

Has a dog inspired you to selflessly serve the greater good?

CHAPTER THREE

A Mission to Heal

A thought transfixed me: for the first time in my life I saw the truth as it is set into song by so many poets, proclaimed as the final wisdom by so many thinkers; the truth — that love is the ultimate and the highest goal to which man can aspire.

— Viktor E. Frankl

Di Thompson
Fredericksburg, Virginia

*S*he was a Christmas gift — sort of; a bedraggled, dirty, malnourished little thing my husband Dan placed in my lap the day after Christmas. He came home late that day, after battling the busy southbound lanes of traffic on Interstate 95 in northern Virginia. He was a retail vice president for Goodwill Industries at the time and had to check on their retail stores before they closed that day.

When he had arrived at his store in Stafford, Virginia, he found the employees huddled around an old, timeworn, wicker basket that someone had stained dark to cover nicks and scars. A small, filthy, black dog lay inside, shivering on a lumpy bed pillow that was covered with an incongruously cheerful flowered pillowcase. The dog was clearly terrified, and worse, she appeared to be injured.

An elderly woman who had gathered with the employees around the basket told my husband that she lived in a nearby trailer park and had wanted to come to the store before it closed. As she had driven out of the park, she had seen a group of young boys wielding sticks and chasing a small dog. She then stopped and scooped up the puppy. One of the dog's eyes was badly injured. She had asked the boys what had happened, but they ran away, leaving her with the dog. She hadn't known what else to do, so she brought the dog into the store.

The woman lived on a fixed income, yet she had bought the secondhand basket and pillow for the dog to lie on. Then she had gone to the grocery store next door and bought a small bag of dog food, dog dishes, and a box of treats. She had brought them back to the Goodwill store and donated them for the puppy. The woman pressed some money into my husband's hand and looked up at him. "Please," she said tearfully, "take this for the dog's veterinary care." Then she turned and left the store.

The employees stood around the basket and watched the woman walk away. The store manager said to Dan, "It's time to close. What should we do with it?"

Dan wanted to say, "Well, why in the world did you accept her?" but he felt so bad about the helpless little dog, his heart melted. I always thought he was a softy when it came to animals, but this was clear proof that, around puppies, his heart was made of marshmallows. Before he could have second thoughts, he tucked the bag of dog things into a corner of the basket, picked it up with the dog cowering in the center of the pillow, and walked to his car.

Bringing Home a Bedraggled Angel

I was sitting in my office at home when Dan plopped the grimy animal in my lap. She was such a pathetic little thing, thin with her ribs clearly visible beneath short, black hair that was dull and matted with mud. She was still shivering. She was young, and it was impossible to tell what kind of dog she might be.

Our aging silver and white Siberian husky, Nikki, immediately inspected the pup from the tip of her nose to the end of her tail, fixed her icy-blue eyes on the small dog, and refused to move more than a few feet away. Her immediate instinct seemed to be to protect this puppy.

I carried the pup to the kitchen and ran several inches of warm water in the sink to give her a much-needed bath. When I gently placed her in the water, her little body relaxed, and she looked up at me with her one good chocolate-brown, adoring eye. I carefully cleaned the other, gouged, eye; placed a small amount of canine antibiotic ointment on it; and put a bandage over it.

Early the next morning, our veterinarian examined the dog and quickly determined that she had been jabbed with something sharp. Her right eye was lost. He guessed her age as approximately six months. I felt ill over the idea that children could do this to an animal. The vet thought she might have some Labrador retriever in her, but he too was at a loss to determine what else she might be. Her ears were quite large for her face, and he guessed that she might be part schipperke or maybe Welsh corgi. Our best hope was that, as she matured, she would give some hints about her heritage. We would never be sure, but it really didn't matter. To us, she was adorable.

We celebrated her birthday on Independence Day, which seemed appropriate now that she was free from any further torment from that pack of boys. There was never really any question about keeping the furry, little black orphan who had fallen into our lives. The only question was what to name her.

Over the next several days, I realized that Nikki and the pup seemed totally devoted to one another. Wherever one went, the other followed. The pup always seemed to be beside Nikki's right-front paw, and they walked in tandem everywhere. When the pup turned, Nikki turned. When the pup stopped, Nikki stopped. If the pup went outside, Nikki stayed beside her.

At age fifteen, Nikki had some arthritis. Her eyes had begun to fail, and she had slowed down considerably. She spent hours each day napping in front of the fireplace in the den or on her big, woolly pillow in my office. Now, with the pup at her side, she was suddenly more active. I marveled at Nikki's newly found confidence to walk around outside in the yard.

A week later, I took the pup back to our vet for a follow-up visit to make sure the blinded eye was healing. It was a beautiful day outside, so I left the patio door open for Nikki in case she needed to go out while I was gone. When we returned home, I found Nikki on the back patio barking in distress. The pup raced out the door onto the patio and positioned herself at Nikki's right-front paw. Nikki instantly stopped barking, and the two walked back together into the house.

Watching this scene made it very clear that Nikki's eyesight had failed far more than I realized and that our one-eyed pup had become Nikki's eyes. She was actually leading Nikki around. This was when we concluded that it seemed right to name the puppy Angel. She had voluntarily assumed the role of Nikki's guardian angel.

Angel's Healing Instincts

When she was younger, one of Nikki's favorite things to do was to ride in our car and visit my mother, who was in her early seventies and bedridden with multiple sclerosis in a nursing facility. I hadn't taken Nikki with me for some time because of the dog's arthritis and the difficulty of getting her in and out of the car. My mother missed Nikki's visits.

Angel's missing eye didn't seem to hinder her navigation in any way. After the injury healed enough to seem safe from infection, I decided to take Angel with me to see my mother.

The facility had two long wings. A rehabilitation wing was on the right, and the left wing contained a full-care, residential nursing facility. My mother's room was on the far end of the residential side, so we had to walk past many rooms. Angel's visit caused quite a stir. She strained against her leash toward most of the residents she saw, trying to get close to them. She seemed to know exactly which residents wanted to pet her and which were reluctant or afraid.

After we reached my mother's room, Angel marched resolutely to her bed, put her paws up on the edge, and looked at me expectantly. I obliged by picking her up and placing her on the bed. Mom was instantly enchanted with the little black dog. Angel cuddled up beside her and stayed there while my mother stroked her for the entire visit.

Di's Angel

Word spread that a dog was visiting, and several residents and staff members came to see her. Angel allowed everyone to pet her but never moved from my mother's side.

From that day on, Angel became a regular visitor to the residential nursing facility. Our arrival was always heralded by a call: "Angel's here!" The announcement echoed down the hallways.

After only a few visits, Angel knew exactly where to go. I could unhook her leash, and she would trot to Mom's room. But first she would stop briefly along the way to allow delighted residents to fuss over her. I would arrive to find Angel already on the bed with Mom.

Angel never wandered into another room or tried to get up on the bed of my mother's roommate, Edna, who must have been at least ninety years old. Edna usually slept while Angel visited my mother. Neither Mom nor I had ever heard her talk, even when she was awake. Nurses told me that Edna was quite feeble and hadn't spoken for a number of years.

One day we arrived at the facility for a visit, and I unhooked Angel's leash. She took off, visiting patients along the way, and turned the corner down the hall to Mom's room. When I caught up to her, she wasn't at my mother's bed. Instead, she had gone directly to Edna's bed, had jumped up on it, and was lying beside the woman's head. Edna was awake, and I immediately became concerned that she might be afraid of dogs or that Angel's claws could inadvertently damage her fragile, papery skin.

I hurried to her side to get Angel off the bed when I saw the most amazing transformation come over Edna's face. Her eyes focused on Angel's face, and she quietly said, "Well, will you look at this? Isn't this the sweetest thing?" She then began talking softly to Angel.

A nurse's aide, who was refilling water pitchers, happened to walk into the room at that moment. She took one look at Edna talking to the dog and ran back into the hall. I thought I would be in trouble for letting Angel get up on the bed.

Two nurses came running in just as I was about to lift Angel from Edna's bed. They quickly stopped me and gestured for me to remain still. We all stood there, watching the frail woman talk to the dog. Angel lay quietly beside Edna with her head on the woman's shoulder. Angel's single brown eye gazed into Edna's sleepy eyes. Within minutes Edna returned to napping. Angel dutifully hopped off Edna's bed and went directly to my mother. Mom spent the rest of our visit snuggled with the dog, as she tenderly stroked Angel's fur.

Now Angel had a new routine when I visited Mom. She would spend a few minutes on Edna's bed, if she was awake, and then would move on to my mother's bed for the rest of the visit. Amazingly, Edna never spoke to anyone else, even her family. Her daughter did not believe the rumor about Angel and Edna until she witnessed one of the visits. Edna passed away a few months later, but her daughter told me she felt that Angel had given her mother a wonderful gift in her final days.

Angel Takes a "Wrong" Turn

Months later, Angel and I arrived at the facility for a routine visit. When I unhooked her leash, she set off down the hallway. Instead of turning left, she inexplicably turned right, toward the rehabilitation wing of the facility. Half a dozen patients in wheelchairs clustered around the nurse's station.

Before any of us could stop her, Angel trotted up to a man who sat slumped and listless in his wheelchair. She placed her paws gently on the seat between his knees. The man raised his head and saw the dog, and his face changed instantly. It was as though someone had aimed a sunbeam at him. He lifted his arms, cupped Angel's face in his hands, and began babbling to her. His words were incoherent, and he smiled at her with only half of his face. The other side of his face was slack and misshapen.

Again, the reaction from the nursing staff was one of disbelief. When I attempted to retrieve the dog, they motioned for me to stop. One of the nurses ran down another hall and returned with a speech therapist, who was astounded that this man was attempting to speak to Angel. The speech therapist told me that this man had recently suffered a stroke and was there for rehabilitation. So far, he had refused all attempts to get him to talk. We let my dog stay with him for a while, and the man chatted happily with Angel for the entire fifteen minutes.

And so, we began yet another new routine for Angel. We visited the rehab wing every time we came. Most of the time, the man who talked only to Angel was there and would light up like a star when he caught sight of her. Each time, his speech became a tiny bit better. One day he wasn't there anymore. Angel turned right and went down the rehab hallway one more time, but she seemed to understand that the man really was gone, so she did not go that way again.

Several weeks later I was sitting in my mother's room with Angel happily snuggled next to her when a woman came to the door. She apologized for interrupting and asked me if this was the little dog who had visited her husband on the rehab side for so many weeks. He had come to the facility feeling deeply depressed, and she had despaired that he would ever get better. She explained that she felt that Angel was the reason her husband had finally begun to rehabilitate. He was now home and progressing well. He was so enamored of Angel that she got him a small, black dog of his own. I was astounded to hear that Angel had made such an impact on this man and his recovery.

Angel's Legacy

Though never formally trained as a therapy dog, Angel instinctively did all the things trained and certified therapy dogs do for people, and she even aided Nikki with her disability. But she gave us no indication when she herself was ill. Angel suffered a sudden heart attack twelve years after she came into our lives. She died quietly beside me in my office, lying peacefully in the woolly bed she had inherited from Nikki.

I remain amazed that, though Angel came to us from such grim beginnings, she never once displayed any animosity or fear of people. She always seemed to know just who needed to touch her, and was quite content to fulfill that need. Despite her dire experience with the boys who blinded her, she loved children and was drawn to them. She was affectionate and loyal and captured the hearts of most everyone who came in contact with her.

The woman from the trailer park, who first brought Angel into our lives, was also a true-blue friend to her. Over the next couple of years when Dan visited the Stafford store, he saw the woman a few more times. She always wanted to know how Angel was doing. One year, in July she left an envelope at the store, addressed to Angel. Inside were a birthday card and a $10 bill with a note to buy Angel a special treat just from her.

Perhaps Angel's greatest contribution can be summed up in a comment one of the staff members at the rehab facility made. As we watched Angel patiently listen to the stroke victim try to talk to her, the staff member said, "That man has a new lease on life through Angel's eyes."

This is Angel's legacy.

MEDITATION

How could the example of a dog or other animal enhance your intuitiveness and help you better trust your sense of inner knowing? Have you observed the gratitude and forgiveness of an abandoned or abused dog who became a friend to humans?

Say a Little Prayer, Renegade

Gail C. Parker
Philadelphia, Pennsylvania

*F*riends of mine, Richard and Jean, wanted me to see Brady, a five-month-old Irish setter from their new litter. I had recently lost my dear Irish setter, Rebel. Richard and Jean told me that November 23 was the birth date of their new litter. This was the same date that Rebel had been born. Although I hadn't planned to adopt another dog right away, when I heard the date of their birth, I had to see the puppies.

As soon as I walked into Richard and Jean's living room, a handsome Irish setter looked right at me, and we bonded immediately. He was so big that I was sure he must've been older than five months and already spoken for. They told me that this dog was actually the brother of Brady, the dog they had picked for me. However, when they saw the way we looked at each other, they knew the dog they called Renny had to be mine. I was already his.

Since Renny was an Irish setter, I wanted to extend the connection to Ireland with an Irish Rebellion theme. The name Renegade popped into my head. When I said it out loud, the puppy took to the new name right away, as if it had been his all along.

Renegade rode on my lap all the way home. To my surprise he knew where everything was in my apartment. It was as if he'd waited for me to come along that April day in 1989.

Renegade Wanted More-Meaningful Work

Because the dog had a wonderful temperament and was quite nice looking, I decided to train him for the show ring. He didn't exhibit that wonderful Irish setter personality when we competed in shows though. According to the breed standard, an Irish setter is supposed to rollick. They are happy, upbeat dogs. Renegade always seemed to want to be anywhere but in the ring. He did the routines for me, but I knew my dog very well. The sparkle was not in him at shows. Also, I am not competitive, which didn't help our performance either. So I decided that showing Renegade was not the path for us.

The Irish setter is an active breed, and these dogs need something to do. The only hunting I did was with my camera, so I had to find another activity for us. At about this time, around 1990, pet therapy was coming into common practice. A friend, Mary Ellen Tarman, encouraged me to try it. I didn't know of any groups in my area that trained therapy dogs, so I wasn't sure what next steps to take.

Since Renegade and I had been to obedience school, I already knew we made a good team and that he was well behaved. From watching him around children and older people in our neighborhood, I could tell that he loved interacting with everyone. Electric cars that children drove on sidewalks, bikes, walkers, wheelchairs, or any other strange city-vehicles didn't faze him. He loved going for car rides, and he behaved like a gentleman in other people's homes. Because I have little depth perception due to blind spots in one eye, Renegade had begun helping me negotiate steps and other places. Observing all of Renegade's characteristics and behaviors caused me to think that he would make an intuitive service dog.

I decided to pray about my decision, and hope for guidance. Shortly after my prayer, a notice appeared in the Sunday bulletin of St. Albert the Great Catholic Church in Huntingdon Valley, Pennsylvania. It asked for volunteers to visit local nursing homes.

After seeing the announcement in church that day, I filled out the application and specified that the nursing home would have to allow me to bring my dog along when I visited. I sent in the form, and the church project's director assigned me to a nursing home. She said that it was up to me to work out with the facility the request for my dog to accompany me.

I made an appointment to meet the nursing home activities director, Yvette. The first thing I saw upon entering the facility was a large sign that read, "We have pet therapy." Talk about getting a sign from above.

The male residents had been asking the staff to please find a big dog to visit them. They considered the little Maltese who lived at the home to be too feminine. So Renegade was the answer to their prayers as much as this nursing home fulfilled my desire to do pet therapy.

The nuns who ran the nursing home welcomed us. Their kindness helped me overcome my feelings of nervousness at trying a new venture. Renegade took to the job immediately. He knew instinctively what to do. He certainly loved this job more than prancing around a show ring.

Renegade's Sacred Service

Whenever we arrived at the home, Renegade and I greeted everyone in the main lobby. Then we headed for the rooms and lounges throughout the home.

To my surprise Renegade always insisted on stopping by the chapel first. He would stand and stare at the altar for a moment. Then, as if finished with his silent prayer, he would indicate readiness to continue our visits. I do not know how Renegade knew that starting with a visit to the chapel would be the proper thing to do, but he did. It was all his idea to start with that little meditation.

Renegade's hunting instincts got a workout on this job. If I asked for a visit with certain residents in the facility, before anyone could tell me where the people were, Renegade found them.

As time passed, I realized that our roles had switched. I was no longer Renegade's handler, as humans were called in obedience class. I was his chauffeur, and Renegade was the therapist. I merely held the leash and let him take the lead. He knew which people only wanted to talk to us and admire him at a distance. He knew which residents liked to merely pet him and which ones also wanted his gentle kisses. He always had a sense of who needed to snuggle with him.

Gail's Renegade

To keep up with my dog and his abilities, I started to read everything I could find about working with people who have physical disabilities. I needed to understand the etiquette for how people in wheelchairs would like to be treated. I learned to relax and talk to the person in the chair, not the attendant pushing it. So many people do not talk to the wheelchair bound, as if they are incapable of intelligent conversation because they cannot walk. I learned to sit, if at all possible. That way, the person in the wheelchair did not have to look up at me in an awkward position for having a chat.

I found out that blind people don't mind if you say, "It is nice to see you." They appreciate when someone offers an arm to help them negotiate difficult terrain. From my Irish setter I discovered that people with disabilities are no different from anyone else. They just have to travel a little differently.

I learned from Renegade that dogs don't care about color, religion, ethnicity, age, ability level, or any other characteristics human beings value. They just want you to be kind. Wouldn't it be great if everyone felt that way? Watching Renegade made me become a better person.

Healing Mrs. H.

One lady at the nursing home, Mrs. H., had had a stroke, and she could be rather nasty at times. She would tell my red dog, "You should run away. Gail is mean to bring you here. Dogs do not belong in a home." She often sat in the lobby and was there when we arrived. People would get up and leave rather than listen to her tirade aimed at me.

In the past, I might have retorted or even ignored Mrs. H. and walked away too. But my dog had taught me that people in the nursing home are worth caring about. So I was nice to her in spite of her jibes. I made sure to smile and say hello, greeting her as warmly as I did everyone else. I'd tell her she was wearing a pretty dress or make a comment about the weather, just to try to interest her in conversation.

One day we entered the lobby, and I noticed that Mrs. H. sat with her back to us. I could see that she had a birthday balloon tied to her wheelchair. I went up to her and wished her a happy birthday and expressed the hope that she would have a really nice day. She was taken aback and thanked me. She even refrained from her usual scolding. After that, she was nicer, and I looked for her during our visits.

On a subsequent visit I couldn't find Mrs. H. in any of the lounges. Renegade led me to a room where we had never visited with Mrs. H. She was in a recliner on wheels, lying still and looking very ill. She saw us at the doorway and motioned for me to come in and lean down to her. She whispered in my ear, "Thank you for visiting me here."

I felt awed and, at the same time, grateful that I had been blessed with this special moment. There are times when a person feels the presence of God, and this moment was one of those times for me.

We never saw Mrs. H. again after that day, because she passed away before we made another visit to the nursing home. Yet her words are written in my heart. They meant more than any trophy or ribbon Renegade and I could have won in that dog show ring.

Renegade's Final Gifts

Renegade did pet therapy for almost ten years. As he neared eleven years old, he developed neurological degenerative myelopathy, which, in dogs, is comparable to multiple sclerosis. There was nothing medically that could be done for him. He had his good days, when he could walk a couple blocks. On the bad days he only wanted to rest on our lawn.

Although Renegade was not in pain, his doctors told me that he would get weaker as the disease took over his body. He developed the laryngeal paralysis that goes along with the disease. This made it difficult for him to breath comfortably. At those times, I eased his throat with a cold pack.

He loved the car and the park, so I would drive as close to the grassy area as I could, and we would enjoy the view. He would lie on the grass while I sat on the low fence. A woman with her elderly Chihuahua often joined us.

On days when Renegade was not able to walk as far as the automobile, we stayed together in the house or on the lawn. I sat outdoors with him while neighbors stopped to visit. They often brought along Renegade's dog friends. I knew that he would let me know when he had had enough of the suffering the illness brought him, but until that time, I was determined to let him enjoy every minute of the time he had left.

Renegade did not want to give up the nursing home visits even after falling ill. He had a wardrobe of neck scarves he only wore for pet therapy. If I took out one of them, he would get all excited and plead to go to work.

I took him for one last trip to the nursing home. I knew that the hill up to the door might be too much for him, but he wanted to say good-bye to his friends so badly that I could not deny fulfilling his wish.

He spent most of the visit lying in front of a man who sat alone in the lobby. He made that man feel so important. Renegade obeyed hand signals from me, so I could let go of his lead. This allowed me to be across the room so the man could have Renegade all to himself that day. Everyone was thrilled that we had done this for the elderly gentleman. But it was Renegade who had known what the man needed.

Our final visit was the only time I ever left the nursing home in tears. I knew how much I would miss Renegade. He had been my teacher, my guide, and my shining example of how people should be.

Not only was Renegade my best friend, but he was also a friend to all in our neighborhood. As Renegade grew frailer, an elderly neighbor he used to visit hobbled with her claw-foot cane across the lawns to see him. She said Renegade had visited her; it was the least she could do to visit him now that he was ill. Later, she confided to me that, although Renegade was gone from this earth, she told her troubles to his framed photograph on her desk, and it made her feel better. Even after his death, my dog was still doing pet therapy.

MEDITATION

How does prayer or quiet reflection prepare you to offer service with an attitude of surrender to your Higher Power?

Tuffy, My Canine Grief-Counseling Partner

Karla Rose, PhD
Boston, Massachusetts

*T*uffy began his work as my K-9 grief-counseling partner when he was just twelve weeks old. Now, at the age of three, he's a full-grown, reddish-orange Cavalier King Charles spaniel. A happy little boy, he sports a thin, white blaze on top of his forehead. He endears himself to everyone — humans and animals — with his huge, round, brown eyes and charming personality.

I adopted Tuffy in August 2004 because of the sadness I felt from my third golden retriever's death a year earlier. My oldest child, Jennie Kate, a freshman at Tufts University, was leaving home. Tuffy became the mascot for the university's field hockey team and traveled to their games every fall for four years. This is how he earned the name Tuffy.

Tuffy and I became a registered Pet Partner team through the Delta Society on his first birthday. Months later, we became certified as a Reading Education Assistance Dogs (R.E.A.D.) team through Intermountain Therapy Animals. Tuffy is trained to read with new or struggling readers, helping them to be more relaxed in a clinical situation or on scene after a tragedy. By having children read to him, Tuffy and I can partner in a unique and less threatening way to assist grieving children or young victims who are witnesses of trauma.

How Tuffy Became a Pet Therapist·

Tuffy and I began visiting cancer patients regularly at the Lahey Clinic Medical Center in Burlington, Massachusetts, during my diagnosis, treatment, and recovery from breast cancer. He was assigned a hospital identification badge that said, "Tuffy — Pet Therapist." I noticed he was especially wonderful at nuzzling with patients in areas where they await mammograms, biopsies, and radiation therapy treatment. He discerns and hones in on those who are sad, exhausted, depressed, or overwhelmed. The staff throughout the hospital stops by the treatment center just to say hello and cuddle this amazing vehicle of love and vessel for stress relief.

Karla's Tuffy

Patients who returned to the hospital for follow-up treatment recalled Tuffy's comfort with affection and gratitude. Each day, upon arrival at the hospital, one patient located the enlarged photo of Tuffy posted at the reception desk. In her daily ritual she paused and touched Tuffy's photo, then methodically outlined the sign of the cross from her forehead to sternum and from left shoulder to right. I understand that many patients did this ritual prior to their treatments.

Knowing that my youngest child, Andrew, would soon leave for college, and having been a single, stay-at-home mother, I began to consider what I might do with my life. I wondered if I could mix my career as a grief and trauma counselor with my love for animals. After Tuffy's extraordinary companionship during my breast cancer, I felt that the experience of taking him to the hospital was God's way of using me as his instrument. Maybe my professional experience and Tuffy's natural healing talents would fuel the next stage of my life and help me find another meaningful way to serve.

Tuffy Helps with Grief Counseling and Trauma Response

While I am a grief and trauma specialist in school and workplace violence, I also have training in disasters and terrorism involving the transportation industry. I started bringing Tuffy to train extensively with local and state police and firefighters, EMTs, and chaplains in Critical Incident Stress Management (CISM). Today, we serve as the canine-clinician members on several Massachusetts CISM teams. This means we are called upon to assist following major crises, such as plane crashes, multiple casualties, fires, and terrorist actions.

The professional work I do requires Tuffy and me to remain calm and provide assistance through all types of crises. I've watched Tuffy stay unflappable under an urgent siege of police and fire sirens, and in the company of barking and aggressing bomb, arson, or drug-sniffing working canines.

Tragedies are traumatic not only for the victims but also for first responders, such as police, firefighters, paramedics, witnesses, hospital workers, and chaplains. As a crisis interventionist, I assist first responders in processing the incident and teach them about some of the emotional, physical, and psychological symptoms they might experience over the next few weeks. Normalizing the symptoms for up to a month following the incident not only reduces the first responders' anxiety but also, it is hoped, prevents flashbacks or other symptoms of post-traumatic stress disorder (PTSD) that could later affect their home or work lives.

In the aftermath of a crisis, withdrawal, isolation, mental confusion, moodiness, and depression are common. But it is essential that people return to experiencing a full range of emotions, including laughing or smiling without feeling guilt or betrayal. Tuffy becomes a loving, nonjudgmental vessel for their bewilderment, tears, or relief. They can express whatever they feel without guilt.

This seventeen pounds of red, silky fur enables them to physically reconnect to the world. The peach, virgin silk that feathers unevenly between Tuffy's toes contrasts with the darker-reddish fur atop his hairy paws. Because his paws make him look like Dr. Seuss's mythical Grinch, Tuffy draws laughter and smiles as people caress him. Feeling the press of his cold nose through a gentle kiss and the touch of his wispy fur soothes their physical, emotional, and spiritual pain. The grieving receive Tuffy's deep gaze that seems to say, "I care so deeply."

As people share words and tears with us, they seek comfort by snuggling Tuffy ever so tenderly. He provides a nonthreatening link, allowing me the opportunity to offer care and reassurance.

It is imperative that those in crisis recall and draw upon coping strategies that were useful in previously difficult times. This gives them a sense of hope and control. I guide them in making a plan for how to find and use external resources during the days and weeks ahead, and provide information for exploring possible referrals so they can get further help, as needed.

Tuffy Prepares for Trauma Work

After I am called to deployment, Tuffy knows what it means if I say, "Ready to go to work, boy!" Tuffy assumes a serious standing posture as we start our routine. He calmly waits as I slip his bulky, multipocketed, monogrammed "Tuffy" CISM vest over his head and snap it closed underneath his belly. In one pocket of the vest he carries our identification with photos and emergency information; another is adorned with protective Christian trinkets that have the images of St. Christopher, St. Francis of Assisi, and the Virgin Mary on them. He follows me patiently as I gather necessary items for our bag, his vest, and credentialing badges. I pack his relaxation nest, a light-green, fluffy bedding pillow that soothes him during his rest periods.

He watches as I prepare the oversized purple backpack that signifies we will work on-site and contains important safety items. I pack glass-, char-, and flame-retardant boots as well as protective eyeware for Tuffy and me, bottled and sterile water, and food and snacks for both of us. The backpack carries a glow-in-the-dark leash, protective goggles, our identifications (with Tuffy's GPS tracking code in case we are separated), and Tuffy's emergency-treatment supplies for fracture, wound, or eye injury. I include a small notebook and pencils, a cell phone, a small radio, a flashlight, and, most important, tissue for the tears that are shed following a tragedy.

Each time we go out to an incident or follow-up, I sit momentarily with Tuffy in my lap, cup his face in my hands, match gazes, and remind him that our mission is to make it better for at least one person by being a caring and compassionate presence.

As we drive to begin our journey to the crisis site, I talk with Tuffy about where we are going and why. Perched forward and safely strapped in his front car seat, he alternates between staring at me and out the windshield. He is purpose-driven en route to our mission.

Tuffy Reports On-Site

Upon arrival, the atmosphere of charged emotions — whether denial, disbelief, or grief — while profound for most humans, inspires Tuffy to hold his head high with a take-charge attitude. I observe a slight kick of pride in each of his steps as he moves onward into the chaos of a situation where violence or disaster has occurred.

On-site we report for directions to the incident commander in charge. At a school incident in the weeks following a tragedy, we seek direction from counselors, office staff, or the school nurse. At the site I watch Tuffy's energy naturally emerge. Never fearful, he advances confidently by my side through the crowd. He seems to have an aura of self-assurance and appears determined to find the group or person who needs him immediately.

When we go to crisis-management briefings, during which the community is informed or updated on an incident, Tuffy assumes a calm presence. He greets the grieving staff or community as they enter and exit the auditorium or meeting area. We sit among those who are suffering the most.

Returning to the Scene

Whether Tuffy circles a dedicated memorial site or visits a counseling area, classroom, campus dining hall, student hangout, or the location of a horrific trauma, his presence brings great comfort. It is as if he invites children and adults who might otherwise be a bit unsure about approaching these places to face their fears with him.

We might be asked to spend time at or near the location of the traumatic incident. Our presence seems to give people permission to revisit a scene and understand the facts (as appropriate) of what happened. This can be helpful in soothing anxiety and physical symptoms. People might relive whatever they saw and felt, and physically respond to the memories by feeling nauseous. I've observed that petting dogs is a powerful way to soothe the vagal nerve, which stimulates or induces vomiting.

At the place where the incident occurred, I often will lay a small quilt on the ground and sit down quietly with Tuffy at my side. Suddenly I might find that thirty or forty people have joined us on the quilt or gathered nearby. They hold Tuffy or embrace each other.

Instinctively, Tuffy rises somberly, walks purposefully, and climbs into the laps of those who seem most upset or sad. He nestles his head into their chests. As despair lightens, without cue, he calmly locates the lap of the next person. He is masterful at climbing up with intention to meet each gaze, as if to say, "I know." An observant clinician likened Tuffy's on-scene comforting behavior to "a hug from a kindly grandmother."

Tuffy perceives the psychological tone of the setting. He becomes solemn when with the saddened. If the mood lightens, perhaps days later, he might ham it up with tricks or "Tuffy just being Tuffy." Smiles return but are often accompanied by momentary guilt or shame, as though a lighter mood were a betrayal of grief and of the loved ones who passed and are missed. Tuffy's antics help to dispel those temporary misgivings and replace them with laughter.

Tuffy Goes to Virginia Tech

My K-9 partner and I were immediately called to assist with the aftermath of the deadliest shooting in the modern-day United States.

It involved the deaths of thirty-two students and faculty on the campus of quiet and pristine Virginia Tech in Blacksburg, Virginia, on April 16, 2007. We were placed on standby status for deployment. On April 23 Tuffy and I responded for one week, beginning our service just as the students and faculty began returning, following the massacre.

I particularly noticed the benefits of pairing therapy canines like Tuffy with grieving college kids after we arrived at the Virginia Tech campus. Separated from their families and pets, the college students welcomed the love sponge who absorbed their grief and gave them comfort. They could cuddle up with Tuffy or shed tears onto his furry body.

Students and other groups we met gratefully expressed that our visit and the time we shared with them was one of the most important healing experiences on campus after the shootings. Tuffy freed them to feel (even if only his fur when they were numb) as they moved cautiously toward recovery.

I felt especially gratified by the warm reception we received in Virginia Tech's dining halls, where we ate with the students. Grieving dining-hall workers wanted to talk or cry, share memories, and express their appreciation for us and to the world for caring so much about Virginia Tech.

On our daily visits to the student union, Tuffy and I sat on the couches with crowds of students. The administration staff, faculty, volunteer counselors, and James Madison University staff volunteers delicately and lovingly hung on the student union walls the many memorial banners that arrived daily. But Tuffy brought to the students the kind of consolation that only a loving dog can deliver.

Watching with great pride and relief, I observed that toward the end of our first week on campus, students began to smile and laugh again. They strove to return to college life as it should be, with swing dancing, marching-band practice, hair braiding, social event planning, relaxation, and calm embraces. Much of this normalcy centered on Tuffy. Perhaps one of the most reassuring things he did was to sleep contentedly amid all the activity within our circle at the student union and bring awareness that life could be peaceful once again.

A memorable event for me was when two women administrators, who had quietly observed Tuffy and me with students in the lounge area, invited us to be the first to see the beautiful and enormous, hand-crocheted American flag that women from North Carolina had made in only a few days. The words they artfully embedded in the corner usually reserved for stars were, "We will never forget — April 16, 2007." The administrators had just received the flag, and they allowed Tuffy and me to hold it with them while we were photographed.

They sent us on our way with their last memorial ribbon pin of Virginia Tech's football team, the Hokies, so we could wear the team's colors with Hokie pride. The goodness of the Virginia Tech Hokies remained palpable throughout the campus. Tuffy wears this memorial ribbon always on his vest with the Hokie bird, a continual reminder to me of "Grace in Action." I treasure the photo, along with crystal memories of faces and words of those thousands of grieving who allowed us the privilege of bearing witness to and sharing their sorrow and grief. They showed Tuffy and me — and the world — their unimaginable faith and optimism during the darkest of days.

Responses to Tuffy

Tuffy's special vest attracted people to us, and they asked why we were there. We were invited to a karaoke gospel sing-along and to a Korean Bible-study group. We attended a sorority prom party that had been planned for over six months.

Everybody was so inquisitive about Tuffy. News spread quickly. When the students got to know us, they sent text messages or called each other to notify others of our location. Wherever we went, we made our presence known first by requesting permission to be there. Everyone was wonderfully receptive and extremely appreciative.

Reflecting back on our experiences, I feel thankful for the immense appreciation kids, teachers, counselors, custodians, first responders, staff, local police, and CISM responders expressed to me in letters, emails, phone calls, and chance conversations. The parents and community residents who were affected directly or indirectly all unequivocally identified one universal theme: Tuffy's loving presence served as a critical bridge from unbearable sadness and grief to healing. We worked long days and evenings, yet Tuffy never grew tired of offering solace.

We touched many lives in our visits to the classrooms, memorial sites, and memorial services, but I feel that we were even more richly touched. Not a day passes that I don't recall faces, conversations, and visions of that campus.

Tuffy Takes On the Tough Jobs

In January 2007, as part of the community's recovery and restoration, we responded to a murder at an affluent high school just west of Boston. We had responded only several months earlier to the premature, sudden deaths of two of the school's recent graduates. As a token of admiration and gratitude for his service, Tuffy was awarded an honorary diploma at the school's commencement and cheered by several thousand celebrants and friends.

Over the years, the media has reported on the grief therapy that Tuffy and I do together. Several editions of the *Boston Globe* featured major articles on our therapy work with cancer patients at Lahey Clinic Medical Center, our trauma response to area schools, and our crisis-response work at Virginia Tech. An ABC-affiliated television station in Boston and newspapers, including a newspaper in Germany, featured our work after the Virginia Tech tragedy. I am gratified over the public's interest and increased understanding of the role a certified therapy dog can play in the devastation that follows a tragedy. But the personal expressions from people whose lives Tuffy has touched bring me the most fulfillment. As a faculty member at Virginia Tech expressed, "Of all the post-trauma resources available, I found the therapy dogs to be the most useful. It is okay to smile at a dog, even when everyone is grieving."

MEDITATION

Has a dog helped you to heal from a deep sorrow? What did the dog do that showed how to listen and comfort someone who is in pain?

Kobi, the Cancer-Detection Dog

Maria Frianeza Rios
San Rafael, California

*O*ur yellow Labrador retriever, Kobi, was three months old when he let me know that, of all the puppies in a litter of twelve, he was determined to go home with me. He cuddled with me and wouldn't leave my side until I got the message.

I thought he was the cutest puppy in the world. Luckily, I had plans to remodel the house, because Kobi decided to chew on everything, including the wall. I did the remodeling after he finished his chewing stage.

Because my employment and commute time keep me away from home for ten hours a day, I enrolled Kobi in a doggy day care that was ten minutes from my home. Kirk Turner, the owner-trainer at the facility, was working with the Pine Street Foundation, an organization in Kentfield, California, that helps people with cancer reach more-informed treatment decisions through education and research. The Pine Street Foundation was conducting groundbreaking clinical-trial research on whether breast cancer and lung cancer could be detected in the breath, and they were using dogs to find out. I told Kirk, "If you ever need another dog for the cancer-sniffing program, you can use Kobi."

When the study needed another house dog, Kobi entered it,

even though he was not yet a year old. He became one of only five pet dogs and service dogs participating in the research; the service dogs were borrowed from Guide Dogs for the Blind. Kobi and the other dogs learned to alert with around 90 percent accuracy after being trained to detect breast cancer and lung cancer in the exhaled breath of cancer patients. In service to early detection, Kobi's nose became a "medical device."

The Pine Street Foundation's website explains the four-month-long research project's reliance on dog cancer-sniffers by stating that a dog's nose is "one of the world's most powerful olfactory sensor[s].... The work is based on the hypothesis that cancer cells emit different metabolic waste products than normal cells. The differences between these metabolic products are apparently so great that they can be detected by a dog's keen sense of smell, even in the early stages of disease....Our study provides compelling evidence that cancers hidden deep within the body can be detected simply by examining the odors of a person's breath."[1]

Although Kobi and the other dogs had no special training in scent discrimination before participating in the double-blind study, they were able to distinguish breath samples of lung-cancer and breast-cancer patients from healthy controls, and help diagnose the disease. After doing his important work in the clinic each day, Kobi came home to be my lovable, playful family dog. This was his mission.

Kobi Hones His Skills

Kobi became excited on the days when he reported for his job. He clearly loved it. When I said, "Kobi, want to go to work?" he'd jump off the bed, bounce up and down, and run downstairs to get into the car. He'd strain his head out the car window, looking for the turns. The dogs in the study were never harmed in any way. They went back to their homes at the end of each day. At the Pine Street Foundation they had constant attention, regular playtime, treats, food, and water.

Maria's Kobi

I would drop Kobi off at the doggy day care early, before going to work. Several times a week, Kirk then drove the dogs to the training and testing site, at a woman volunteer's big guesthouse. At the end of the day I would pick up Kobi at day care.

Kobi was quick to learn what would be required of him and became very enthusiastic. The trainers used clicker training (making a clicking sound that the dogs learned to recognize as an indicator that they had done the right thing), followed by positive reinforcement and rewards. The testers would line up five samples in a row. When a dog found the one from a cancer patient, he would sit in front of it.

The samples were from people who breathed into a polypropylene, organic vapor-sampling tube that had a synthetic "wool" to capture organic compounds in exhaled breath. People who had recently been diagnosed with lung or breast cancer and healthy people provided breath samples. The breath samples were in a plastic container with holes poked on top so the dogs could sniff the scent without disturbing the sample.

The actual data that the Pine Street Foundation published came from the double-blind test phase. Nobody in the room knew the identity of the samples. The dogs' responses were simply recorded (for example, "Dog sat in front of sample #2") and then later evaluated. No praise was given during the test phase of the research.

Kobi was such a cute dog and funny to watch. Everybody loved him, and they were amazed at his accuracy. As soon as he found a cancer sample, the trainer would click and reward him with a treat. Kobi would sometimes run back to a positive sample again in hopes of getting yet another treat. The trainers had to take hold of his collar so he'd know to stop doing that.

Kobi sniffed the cancer samples really fast and with so much confidence. He didn't take his time. After all, he knew that there was a treat at the end. At first, he would sniff each of the samples and then pick out the one that was from a cancer patient. Later, he would sniff the positive sample and stop without continuing on to sniff the others. He was amazing. Whenever I picked him up after his training, the researchers and Kirk said that Kobi did a fantastic job. He was one of the higher-achieving dogs.

Kobi Takes His New Skill Home

Having Kobi become skilled at detecting cancer put me in a tough position. One person asked if she could come over to my house to see Kobi because she thought she might have cancer. I was hesitant about allowing him to do that. On the Pine Street Foundation's website, in the "Frequently Asked Questions" section, one of the questions is whether anyone could train a dog to detect cancer, which raises ethical and moral issues about such things as whether the results could be trusted.[2] Might the dog give a false positive or negative? Assuming the dog didn't give a false positive, what type of cancer might the person have? That information would be important for a patient to know, but the dogs wouldn't be able to tell.

Once in a while we went to a dog park, and Kobi honed in on a person and barked. The Pine Street Foundation's study results hadn't been published yet. It was a moral dilemma, because I didn't want to alarm someone by saying that Kobi thought the person might have cancer. It's my understanding that the dogs can detect cancer even before medical equipment and tests can diagnose it. The person Kobi identified might get tested medically but be at a too-early stage for cancer diagnosis and therefore think nothing was wrong.

Kobi had met my brother's mother-in-law and hadn't reacted to her. Then she was diagnosed with ovarian cancer about the same time that Kobi joined the research project. Ordinarily Kobi is mellow all the time and doesn't bark unless someone is at the door. The next time he saw the woman who had ovarian cancer, he wouldn't stop barking at her. He followed her through the house and even continued to bark when she closed the door and went into a different room. She passed away within a few weeks of meeting Kobi.

Kobi Becomes Famous

After the Pine Street Foundation published its research findings in the *Integrative Cancer Therapies* journal,[3] the organization began a media blitz. It had been a couple of years since the testers had trained Kobi to locate the smells and about a year since he'd had the chance to do it again. We had to do a refresher practice before we filmed the process for the nationally televised *Today* show. Still, Kobi found the cancer samples 100 percent of the time for his national television demonstration.

The research results received a lot of media attention, including coverage by the *New York Times*, CNN, *Parade* and *Prevention* magazines, the BBC, and the Discovery Channel. International television stations from Japan, China, and Chile, among others, came to film Kobi.

I had been banned from observing Kobi's training to detect cancer, because the researchers thought it would distract him if he knew I was nearby. But a year before the research report was published, I had to take Kobi for a BBC filming about the project. Kobi's trainer wasn't at the filming, so I hid behind a curtain to watch. They let Kobi go, and instead of finding the cancer sample, he headed straight for the curtain. It was like exposing the Wizard of Oz. He just sat there wagging his tail, as if to say, "Oh good, you're watching me!" After he did that, I had to leave the property, so I never got a chance to watch his demonstration. I heard later that Kobi nailed it and got everything right.

On another occasion, when we took Kobi to the Pine Street Foundation clinic the day before filming the *Today* show, the samples were a year or two old at that time. We weren't sure if the breath smells would still be strong enough for him to detect cancer. But Kobi found every cancer sample. The guys at the clinic called him "Master Kobi," because he was so good at the job.

Kobi's Untimely Passing

Kobi started coughing in the middle of the media blitz, so I took him to our veterinarian, who gave him antibiotics. After a couple of weeks, the cough didn't go away, so the vet took X-rays. Ironically Kobi had lymphoma.

We tried everything we could to save Kobi's life. The Pine Street Foundation helped us a lot. They even recommended acupuncture and some herbs used for human cancer patients.

Kobi was only three years old when he got cancer. He had been completely healthy. The disease progressed very fast. I researched what I could do to help him and read books about dogs who beat cancer. I tried to answer the question of whether we should have Kobi go through chemo or die naturally. His lifespan was supposed to have been only six months without treatment.

Within two weeks of his diagnosis, only a few weeks before my birthday, in March 2006 — the same month the research paper was published — Kobi passed away due to complications from the chemotherapy treatment, not the cancer. To me it is somewhat of a cruel irony that Kobi died after his second chemotherapy session to abate the cancer in his own body. Cancer is not contagious, so I don't think there is a link between his sniffing and getting the disease.

Grieving Over Kobi

It makes me sad that Kobi died after only two weeks of the therapy. If he had not done the chemo, I would have had him for another six months. My only consolation is that he didn't have to suffer. He hated taking medications and going to the veterinarian's office. He was very sensitive, and being sick made him depressed.

When I was growing up we had pets, but none of them were really mine. I don't have any children, so Kobi was my baby, my first dog, my pet soul mate. We did everything together. My mom would tell my dad, "I really want a human grandchild, not a dog grandchild."

Kobi's passing was devastating for my fiancé, Richard, and me. At the time of Kobi's illness, Richard was on disability and stayed at home with Kobi. Those two were inseparable. Now our house was empty. I could escape by going to work for a while, but Richard and I both slipped into depression.

We do feel that Kobi is still in the house spiritually, even though his physical body is gone. Soon after he passed away, I awoke in the middle of the night, because I felt that I had heard Kobi circling in the room and plopping down. I didn't think anything of it, but the next morning, I told Richard that I'd heard Kobi. He said that he'd heard exactly the same sounds that night.

My future mother-in-law used to dog-sit with Kobi when I was out of town, and she came with us to the hospital to visit Kobi on the day before he died. After Kobi was gone, she was at our home lying in bed when she heard Kobi's distinctive big sigh from the side of her bed. Her experience added to my sense that Kobi remained with us.

When Kobi was alive, he always looked through the glass front door so he could see us coming home. One time after Kobi's death, I threw open the front door, but it ricocheted back, even though it hadn't hit anything solid. This threw me off guard. It was as if the door had hit the spot where Kobi used to lie and he was present there.

Kobi's Legacy

We invited people who were special to Kobi to attend his burial. The people at the Pine Street Foundation were so sweet. They named a star after Kobi with the International Star Registry. They called it "Master Kobi, Scientist and Friend." Kobi is part of a group in the Canine Stars.

I buried Kobi at a pet cemetery in Napa on gorgeous property. Richard and I visit his grave often. We talk to him every day, so he knows we plan to move from the home where we lived with him. We say, "Kobi, make sure you come to stay with us."

After Kobi passed away, we asked all the people who had done the filming and taken pictures if we could have raw footage for our memories. An NBC cameraman took the extra time and effort to put together a montage of footage and accompanied it with music.

Seven and a half months after Kobi died, Richard and I wedded. We used the video from the NBC cameraman for the first dance during our reception. We had always wanted Kobi to be ring bearer, but he passed away before that could happen. Because of the video, Kobi was with us when we began married life. We felt very emotional while watching it.

For us, it was such an honor to have Kobi as part of our lives, because we know the study will help people. The Pine Street Foundation is getting grants from the Department of Defense and other funders to find out which chemicals Kobi and the cancer-sniffing dogs were finding in the samples. They are going forward with a lot of projects to aid in early detection. This could mean saving thousands of lives and finally getting some sort of attack plan against cancer. I have friends with cancer. Everybody knows at least one person who has it. I feel proud to know that Kobi has been part of this huge project. If the scientists can develop something from what they learned through Kobi's work, that makes his life even more meaningful.

Even though it has been almost two years since Kobi died, his legacy continues. I still get calls from people who are writing about him in research papers. He has touched many lives. One of the best cards we received was from an eight-year-old girl. She wrote to us about how much Kobi influenced her with his hard work and dedication. She said that she loves him.

Although we were always proud of Kobi's important work, when he came home, he was still our baby. We knew him as a fun dog with a quirky personality. He was very particular. For example, he wouldn't jump on our bed if his blanket wasn't there. He wouldn't jump in the car until we moved things out of his way. Everything needed to be orderly for him to settle down and sleep with us. Those are the little things I miss the most. His carefulness at ensuring that he had things exactly right made him good at what he did at the Pine Street Foundation's clinic.

How could a three-year-old dog have such a positive impact on the world? He was my house dog, my puppy. We ran in the park every day. But Kobi had a bigger job, and because he performed it successfully, his life made an impact.

MEDITATION

Could a dog's contribution to your life be something you can find a way to honor, even as you grieve over your losses?

CHAPTER FOUR

A Mission to Protect

One thing that dogs sometimes don't get from us is respect for their dogness. The magic of our enduring partnership lies in the fact that we are two such different species. We diminish that magic when we treat dogs like four-legged people, or babies, or even toys. We come closest to knowing our dogs when we remember their wild instincts, and the strengths and senses they inherit from those wolves who crept up to our cooking fires so many thousands of years ago.

— Gena K. Gorrell

The Dogs of War

Lt. Col. Christopher P. Coppola, USAF
San Antonio, Texas

*I*n my job as a military trauma surgeon, I have twice been deployed to the Air Force Theater Hospital in Balad, Iraq. I see all sorts of life-threatening injuries in civilians and troops. Military dog teams have also been brought to our hospital several times. Because of these encounters, I have observed firsthand incredible examples of selflessness and bravery, not only in troops and civilians but also in the human-canine teams.

One of the most fascinating bonds between dogs and humans is the relationship between military working dogs and their handlers. Each branch of the military has its military working-dog teams, and there are 578 in the Army alone. Many military working-dog teams have been deployed to Iraq in support of Operation Iraqi Freedom. Every day, the dogs and handlers train extensively and function in close cooperation with each other. If a central kennel is not available for the dogs, the teams are even housed together. They share a special bond that allows them to function in unison.

Military working dogs are selected as puppies and undergo extensive training at military facilities before they are able to enter service in a war zone. At Lackland Air Force Base in San Antonio, Texas, for example, litters of puppies are born on the base and stay with their mothers until they are old enough to live with an adoptive family. Families provide foster homes for the pups with the understanding that they must give up the dogs if they turn out to have the right stuff to become military working dogs. When the dogs are approximately six months old, they return to the base to undergo testing. They must have a high degree of discipline to perform in a war zone. Most dogs do not pass the tests. They return to the families that raised them from pups and are permanently adopted.

Military working-dog teams serve many important functions in Iraq that keep the troops safe. They protect borders and gates to keep forward-operating bases secure. U.S. troops in Iraq are stationed at these forward-operating bases across the country, which serve as safe havens for launching missions. Dogs also help to search out concealed enemy combatants who could be a threat to civilians and troops. Dogs with additional specialized training detect concealed explosives or weapons. The dog-handler teams need the same courage and dedication as any troops deployed to the war zone. Military dogs function with absolute bravery and obedience. Their handlers have the ultimate responsibility of protecting the dogs' lives, because, in turn, these dogs will save the lives of others.

The Injured Partners

One day in 2007, our combat-support hospital received a unique pair of patients. We treated a military working-dog team that had been injured by an improvised explosive device. Their team had been hunting concealed explosives to protect other troops. The soldier paid no mind to his pain and injuries, as we washed and dressed his several small wounds. His only thoughts were for his dog. He asked us to please take care of his dog first.

The dog was a young German shepherd with powerful muscles under a shiny coat marked with dust and blood. Our emergency room in Balad is a broad, clean, white room divided into bays to accommodate seriously injured patients. It can quickly go from a quiet scene of medical technicians restocking equipment to the controlled chaos of caring for people with multiple casualties whose lives hang in the balance. Our team of doctors, nurses, and technicians works in unison to quickly diagnose and treat battle-injured troops and civilians. Our emergency room can rival the trauma capabilities of any major metropolitan hospital.

Witnessing the close bond between this dog and his handler that day gave a new spiritual quality to the utilitarian environment of our emergency room. Many hospital personnel flocked around the pair, perhaps out of curiosity or because their minds turned to their own pets back home.

The soldier, lying on a stretcher adjacent to his dog's, asked us to do whatever we could to save his partner's life. The canine had taken a fragment to the neck. He lay on the stretcher, breathing quickly. Blood had soaked through the bandage wrapped loosely around the dog's neck. The handler spoke softly, telling his dog partner that he was a good boy and had done a good job.

We examined the injured animal's wound, replaced his dressing, and controlled the bleeding. The entire time we examined the dog, he stayed calm and cooperative. He allowed the emergency room doctor and technician to do their work without any protest. After the dog's and handler's wounds were tended to, this brave team evacuated together from Iraq for further treatment.

The Dogs Who Don't Return to Work

Another day, a military working dog suffered a stroke and was brought to our hospital. He was not very old and had served actively up until the time of his illness. His handler told us that he had been such an eager and active dog. It pained him to see the dog reduced to this state. The dog remained aware but was weakened to the point where he could not rise up off the stretcher. Although it must have been frightening to the dog, it is a credit to his training that he remained calm in the foreign environment of our hospital. Though he moved little, his eyes seemed to follow each member of our team as they approached him.

His handler understood that we couldn't undo the damage done by the dog's stroke, yet he still expressed his gratitude to us. He told us he planned to accompany the dog back to the veterinarians at their home station. Even though the dog would no longer be able to serve in the military, his handler wanted to remain with him. After the dog arrived back in the United States and had been released from the canine corps, his handler planned to adopt and continue caring for him.

The most tragic event we saw befall a military working-dog team was when a dog came to our hospital with seizures. The dog was a young Staffordshire-terrier mix with a brindled coat. A new arrival to the theater of operations in the war zone, he and his handler had recently been deployed to service in Iraq and were just getting accustomed to their new quarters and the kennel.

The team was trained to detect explosives. They were doing additional training, as the handler tested his dog's ability to detect a plastic explosive called C4. He hid a small amount of C4 in the training area. His dog rapidly found the C4, but unfortunately, he consumed some of it. C4 is highly poisonous, and even that tiny amount could be a lethal dose. The kennel veterinarians couldn't do anything for him. They sent the dog to us as a last-ditch effort.

The pitiful animal twitched as his strength faded. He drooled and his eyes were unfocused as his breathing became shallow and irregular. His handler couldn't have been more than twenty-three years old. The soldier could barely hold back his tears, and the muscles of his square-set jaw clenched. He stroked the fur of his dog's face and spoke to him softly, telling him it was going to be all right. None of us could do anything except try to make the dog comfortable and give him fluids to dilute the effects of the poison.

His handler was inconsolable. He stayed by his canine partner through the treatment. I could tell by the look in the soldier's eyes that his heart ached. It was clear that the dog meant more to this young man than just being a highly skilled and trained animal. The two had prepared for war together, and shared a closeness and dependence on each other. With the close attention of our staff and the veterinarians, fortunately the dog was able to pull through.

Together in Action

The conflict in Iraq has seen the first military working-dog team killed together in combat since the Vietnam War. On July 6, 2007, military working-dog Cooper and his handler Corporal Kory Wiens were killed together while on duty. They were part of the First Engineer Brigade, Fifth Engineer Battalion, Ninety-fourth Mine Dog Detachment.

Cooper was a four-year-old Labrador retriever, and Corporal

Wiens was twenty years old. As part of a specialized team capable of finding hidden munitions and explosives, Cooper had been trained to work in the war zone without a leash. The team was on patrol together in Muhammad Sath, Iraq. Both dog and handler were killed when an improvised explosive device detonated.

Corporal Wiens's family chose to honor their son and the dog's special relationship by burying them together in Wiens's hometown, Dallas, Oregon. At a memorial service honoring Corporal Wiens and Cooper, thirty-seven working-dog teams marched, including teams from the Army, Navy, Air Force, Marines, and local police.

Together Forever

Military working dogs are so close to their handlers that the dogs can have a therapeutic effect when they are needed. When Tech. Sergeant Jamie Dana from the Twenty-first Security Forces Squadron dog handlers was injured in Iraq, her military working dog, Rex, was with her. Rex, a five-year-old German shepherd, had also served with Sergeant Dana in Pakistan. She was traveling near Kirkuk on June 25, 2005, when an improvised explosive device destroyed the HMMWV (High-Mobility Multipurpose Wheeled Vehicle, known as Humvee) in which she was riding. Sergeant Dana was seriously injured, but Rex suffered only a small burn on his nose. The soldier underwent emergency surgery and received nineteen blood transfusions. A medic mistakenly told her that Rex had been killed in the explosion.

Later, Sergeant Dana was evacuated from Iraq to Landstuhl Regional Medical Center in Germany and then on to Walter Reed

Medical Center in Washington, D.C. While in Walter Reed, she discovered that Rex had survived, so a visit was arranged.

Rex ran into her room and leaped onto Sergeant Dana's bed. Sergeant Dana now knew that her best friend was okay and that she herself would make it. Sergeant Jamie Dana recovered and retired, but Rex was able to continue serving as a military working dog. After an outpouring of public support and passage of a bill in Congress, Sergeant Dana was able to adopt Rex on January 13, 2006, and continue her recuperation at home with her dog.

Friendly Heroes

During my deployment to Iraq in late 2007, I went to visit the kennel for military working dogs on Logistical Support Area Anaconda in Balad, Iraq. In addition to housing, the dogs have exercise and training areas that are protected from the rest of the base. There are air-conditioned enclosures to keep the dogs cool in the Iraqi heat, as well as offices and a kitchen for preparing the dogs' meals. The facility is home to dogs from all of the military services, because they rotate deployments to central Iraq. There is a staff of veterinarians who provide for the dogs' health needs and inspect their food to make sure no one has poisoned it.

I got to meet with the kennel master to talk with him about the facility. He brought one of the dogs out with him. She was a playful six-year-old German shepherd named Isis, who immediately ran over to me to say hello.

I sat down on the floor to play with Isis, and she licked my face.

Lt. Col. Coppola and Isis

All of the military police officers in the Provost Marshal's office next door to the kennel knew her. They said that she was one of the friendliest dogs they had met. Since I had been away from my family and our dog after being deployed to Iraq, it was a great thrill to get to play with such a friendly dog for a few minutes. These military working dogs may be canine heroes, but that doesn't stop them from being loving companions too. It amazes me to observe individuals, both dogs and humans, focusing on the good of their team members and the mission, even in the face of severe pain or danger.

MEDITATION

Who are the heroes in your life? Are any of them dogs? What are the acts of courage they have done that inspire you to greater sacrifice and service?

The Little Mother Who Saved My Life

Rebecca Kragnes
Minneapolis, Minnesota

*T*hroughout my life I had never experienced the incredible bond that can develop between animal and human, and I was definitely afraid of dogs. Animals were soft, but dog paws could jump up and scratch me. Animals also had teeth that might do all sorts of damage. Some animals emitted unpleasant odors, and this was another reason I avoided them.

Consequently instructors at the Seeing Eye®, Inc., the organization based in Morristown, New Jersey, that trains dog guides for the blind, had an uphill battle trying to get me to love a dog. For an introduction to my first dog guide, Tanner, the staff at the Seeing Eye bathed and sprayed the golden retriever with doggy cologne. They warned me that he licked and said we'd work on that. After a couple of days of training with Tanner, I stopped washing my hands every time he licked them. Within another week, I praised him without hesitation by saying "good boy," even though I knew the praise would result in one of Tanner's licks.

But the deeper bonding took place while we worked in real-life situations. I knew that I couldn't take Tanner home if I hadn't come to trust him on the street. It was his outstanding performance in harness that won me over. His abilities to go around obstacles and stop before climbing up or walking down stairs amazed me. I found myself developing a much brighter view of the world through working with Tanner.

We had a small setback after going home from the Seeing Eye training facility. Because I frightened easily if other dogs barked, Tanner felt that he had to defend my honor and would start barking back at the dogs. I became afraid of him at these times and wondered if he might turn on me. A visit from an instructor, who assured me that Tanner would never hurt me, got us back on track.

Tanner was only six years old when the devastating day came when I had to euthanize him to spare him from pain. I knew something was wrong when he avoided and even hid from his food, since eating was among his favorite things to do. Tanner had intolerable pain, but it took another month for the veterinarians to make the diagnosis of kidney failure.

Shelly Didn't Like the Job

Still grieving Tanner's passing for a year, I tried to work with my second golden-retriever dog guide, Shelly. After nine months of unsafe travel and behavioral problems, it was apparent that Shelly just didn't like her job. She did okay at following my husband, Phil, and his German-shepherd dog guide, Wanetta, but when we worked by ourselves, she'd freeze. Nothing I did could get her to go. Once, it took me half an hour to get through a door with her. I had to start building in extra time to go from place to place, yet her freezing episodes continued to make us late for appointments.

Shelly also tried to take dangerous shortcuts to hurry home and get out of her harness. Even after coming inside from having had a chance to relieve herself, she would have accidents in the house and run away from them. Ultimately I had to send Shelly back to the Seeing Eye for reevaluation.

Maternal Wynell

By now, I had lost two dog guides in a year, and my confidence in working with a dog was at an all-time low. The most promising dogs are bred for a couple of years before being trained as guides.

When the Seeing Eye said they didn't have a young dog for me, I wondered what they meant. They told me about a retired breeder dog, a four-year-old golden retriever. This dog had just finished training as a dog guide, and the trainers felt she would be perfect for me. After all of Shelly's behavioral problems, I looked forward to the maturity of a dog named Wynell.

I had traveled to the Seeing Eye training facility in Morristown to get Tanner and Shelly. This time, an instruc-

Rebecca's Wynell

tor brought Wynell to me for home training. That arrangement boosted my confidence a notch, because I knew the area and planned routes during training to familiarize Wynell with regular places we would travel to.

I was amazed when I walked with Wynell for the first time. She used just the right amount of pull on her leash and showed the work ethic I needed. Wynell had a calm presence and didn't run away, as Shelly had done, whenever I dropped something. To me, she was like an angel from God. Little did I know how prophetic my thoughts about her would be.

A friend of mine watched Wynell work and started calling her "the little mother." The name fit because of Wynell's former breeding-dog status and the care she exhibited with me.

Wynell to the Rescue

Feeling gratitude and peace for my dog guide, I walked home from the bus stop on a warm, sunny February afternoon with Wynell. At this time, she had been with me for a year and five days, and was giving me new self-assurance. She had been checked by the veterinarian for a sore throat that day, and I'd seen a doctor for my cough. My husband was recovering from quadruple-bypass surgery, so I needed to get home to feed both Wanetta and Wynell.

Soon, Wynell and I came upon a wide street. I listened carefully, and when the parallel traffic began — my signal that the light had turned green — I said, "Wynell, forward."

We began to cross. Three quarters of the way across the street, I suddenly felt Wynell jerk back violently before the world went gray. Although we had crossed correctly, a driver hadn't seen us and had made a quick turn onto the street.

I awoke with the taste of vomit in my mouth. Hands lifted me into an ambulance. I panicked when I thought that Wynell was missing. Had she gone out into the busy street and been killed?

Later, I learned that, despite my inability to control her after being hit by the car, Wynell had maternally stayed with me. A policeman had examined her while the EMTs put me in the ambulance. She had bounded into the ambulance to hover as close to me as possible. At last, I felt the warm sensation of her licking my skin to make sure I was okay.

Afterward, I described the accident to a trainer from the Seeing Eye. He told me that it was very likely that Wynell had saved my life. By jerking me far enough back from the car, its impact had been minimized.

My injuries were substantial, but luckily, I could walk. Wynell received only a scratch on her paw. My biggest worry was whether she would ever guide for me again. Sometimes accidents can traumatize dogs, rendering them unable to work.

The day I took my first walk after the accident, it was icy. I asked a police officer to go with me in case anything went wrong. Wynell slowed down and guided me carefully through the rough terrain. She remained even more vigilant of traffic than before my injury as she continued her role of being the little mother in my life.

Wynell, a Family Dog

We had many adventures in the five and a half years that Wynell served as my smart, sweet Seeing Eye Dog®. She was calm and quiet in her harness, even when I permitted others to pet her. After the harness came off, she definitely knew she was off duty. She was much more wiggly and a social butterfly. She'd bark when the doorbell rang, but she tried to be the first to greet our guests by squeaking and bringing a gift in her mouth of a shoe or bone.

Wynell was my foot warmer by the fireplace on long winter nights. She loved when I scratched the sides of her muzzle by her ears. She would run toward our freezer whenever she heard us working with ice, because we'd give her at least one piece. Her beautiful work and loving presence healed past hurts and enriched my life immeasurably.

Retiring Wynell

As Wynell neared her tenth birthday, it was not an easy decision, but I realized that I must have her retired. She worked her best, but I knew that her heart simply wasn't in it anymore. Wynell reminded me of how Shelly had shown her reluctance to work by suddenly freezing rather than finding a way around an obstacle. The longer I kept Wynell in service, the guiltier I felt.

It just wouldn't have felt right for me to leave her alone at home while I trained and worked with my next dog guide. I admire people who can keep their retired dog guides as pets, but it's not for me.

I began trying to find a retirement home for Wynell. I wanted a situation in which she would be with people almost all the time, as she had been with me. I also wanted her to be with other animals because of her happy relationship with Wanetta. I knew she needed the companionship of other dogs.

A few years ago, I thought I had everything figured out for Wynell's ideal retirement. A friend who stayed home most of the day and had other animals said she wanted her. Then, last year my friend decided to work outside of the home.

I credit God with what happened next. During my hotline volunteer work for a golden-retriever rescue organization, a woman named Jere (pronounced "Jerry") called to ask a specific question about fostering. She and her family had lost a special golden retriever named Snickers. They wanted to foster older goldens in his memory. I decided to tell Jere my story about Wynell and the dog's need for a loving home.

Jere quickly forwarded photos of Wynell to her grown daughters and discussed our circumstances with them. That night, Jere, a daughter, and a granddaughter came to our house to see Wynell. Jere warned me that for months the grieving family couldn't look at a golden retriever without crying.

While Wynell met Jere and her family on our porch, the adults' tears flowed. The young granddaughter said that she missed Snickers. We introduced Wynell to Jere's other two dogs. Wynell was ready to say hi, and she and Trip, the white, female mixed-breed dog, became fast friends. Big, the male, black poodle, wasn't so sure at first and backed away. By the end of the evening, though, I was certain I had found the perfect place for Wynell.

Jere and I talked by phone several times that weekend. She said that her granddaughter couldn't stop chattering about Wynell. I had Wynell's records faxed to the office of Jere's veterinarian. Then we began to plan for Wynell's last days with me.

In the days preceding Wynell's retirement, Phil and I were probably a little more lax about correcting her when she licked crumbs off our table. We said, "You're going to have a harder time doing that in your new home with people who can see, so you'd better get it out of your system now!"

On the day Wynell was to start her new life, I gathered all of the things I had planned to send with her and put them in a sack. My packing her food bowl alerted Wynell that she was going on a trip, but I don't think she understood that she would no longer call our house her home. I paused at the threshold of our door with tears in my eyes and left for the last time with Wynell guiding me.

Jere met us at an agency for the blind. There was an awful storm that day, with watches and warnings everywhere in the area. Jere's home was an hour's drive away. We discussed several alternatives to the unworkable plan we had made for me to go with Wynell to Jere's home so that I could later imagine where she lived. Understandably Jere didn't want to drive any more than necessary in the storm. She offered to take us home and put off the retirement until another day. Since the emotional buildup had been intense for everyone, I decided that we needed Wynell's transfer to happen right then and there.

At the entrance to the building, I took off Wynell's harness, leash, and collar. Jere put a different collar and leash on her. We tearfully hugged with Wynell between us. Then Jere hustled Wynell to her car so that she wouldn't have to see me leave in a cab without her.

I felt empty on the way home. I shared a taxi with another woman and her dog guide, because the cab company didn't want to send out more than one vehicle in the stormy weather. I had to work very hard to keep from screaming as the woman lovingly interacted with her dog in the backseat. I managed to keep most of my tears in check until I arrived home.

Wynell, the Wise Healer and Teacher

Jere and I continued to stay in touch. I was happy and comforted to hear that Wynell got along beautifully with everyone. No longer do Jere's family members cry over the loss of Snickers when they see Wynell or any other golden retriever. She has healed their past hurts, as she did mine.

Though I'm at peace about retiring Wynell, I miss not having a dog guide. A cane can't show me places we've been before, alert me to people and obstacles without hitting them, and guide me from ramp to ramp when crossing a street. Only a dog guide reacts to changes in the environment, understands instructions, and guides accordingly.

When my new dog guide arrives, he or she will need time to learn all these things about working with me. I can give the dog the time required to learn everything necessary for my protection.

My only wish is for Wynell to enjoy her golden years. Hopefully, once I meet and train with my next dog, I'll find happiness again too. Perhaps Wynell and I will be able to see each other one day. I would love to meet the rest of her family and experience Wynell's new home. I hope she will pass on her wisdom to her successor. Until then, farewell, Wynell.

MEDITATION

Have you ever been reluctant to let a dog or other animal, or a person into your life, only to discover that he or she brought unexpected gifts and blessings?

How Scooby-Doo Earned His Angel Wings

Anna and Neman Bates
Cherryville, North Carolina

*L*ife is full of surprises when you bring home a tiny six-week-old puppy who will grow up to be a 170-pound Great Dane. At first, puppy Scooby-Doo (also known as Scooby) was smaller than our two tabby cats, Schitz and Chaos. From the beginning we noticed that he had a special place in, and knew the meaning of, family. He grieved when Chaos passed away from kidney failure. Chaos used to lick the inside of Scooby's ear.

One of Scooby's favorite poses was to lie beside us with his paws wrapped around our legs, as if to say, "I belong with you. You belong to me." His smart, sweet, and clumsy personality combined the cartoon characters Scooby-Doo and Marmaduke, both of whom were Great Danes.

By the time he was grown, Scooby-Doo had dark-blond hair and a huge head with a soft, squishy black mouth that wet with drool and covered our faces with sloppy kisses. Scooby-Doo didn't settle for a kiss on the cheek though. It was either a kiss right on the front of the face, with our permission, or he might offer a sneak-attack kiss when we least expected it, just to make us smile. He was so big that, if he stood beside us as we sat at a table, he was taller than we were. Scooby transformed from a lovable puppy into the most affectionate and funny dog, who enjoyed nothing more than having our full attention.

Scooby understands emotions and joins in on whatever we are feeling. Those moments when any of us is sad become an open invitation for him to push his big, wet nose up to our noses or mouths and give sincere little licks. When our family is being goofy and playing around, Scooby always gets excited and runs through the house. The only problem is that when he puts his brakes on and skids to a halt at the end of our long hallway, the carpet curls up under his weight. Neman named this act "the rodeo clown." Because Scooby can't contain his exuberance while we laugh at him, he starts bucking like a clown riding a bronco in a rodeo as he continues to run.

Scooby was ten months old when Anna became pregnant with our son, Zen. Scooby would come near her, and she'd point to her stomach and say, "Easy. The baby is in here." Anna believed he knew what she meant, because every time she said those words to him, he'd kiss the outside of her shirt as if to show affection for the baby in her womb. He also liked to lie near her abdomen during those months when the baby grew inside of her.

Scooby became very watchful of our house while Anna was pregnant. He would run out the door when we opened it and bark at the woods, as if declaring, "You'd better not come into my yard." Yet Scooby welcomed everyone we invited into our home.

After Zen was born, Scooby was so good with him. Picture a huge dog hovering over a little baby. He was gentle and kissed the baby. Ever careful, Scooby stayed with Zen much of the time, always protecting the infant (while under our supervision, of course).

Scooby seemed content with just about anything Zen wanted to do, as long as it made us happy. It was precious to watch Scooby tend to Zen as if he were his very own child. When Zen was a toddler, he and Scooby played horse with our tiny cowboy riding him and bouncing up and down on the dog's back. After these sessions, the two rested and eventually fell asleep, with Zen nestling his little body against Scooby's enormous side.

Scooby-Doo Becomes Our Hero

By the time Zen was two and a half years old, if we needed to be at work early the next morning, we occasionally had him picked up at eight thirty in the evening to spend the night with his grandmother, whom he calls Nana. On June 18, 2007, at four thirty in the morning, our house caught fire due to an electrical shortage in the sunroom. We were most grateful that this was one of those nights when Zen was not at home.

We woke up to Scooby's jumping on our water bed. He batted at us with his big paws and barked frantically. This was unusual. After he burst our mattress a few years earlier and water poured out of it, Scooby had never again jumped on our water bed, even though his bed lay next to ours.

But that morning Scooby repeatedly hurled his body onto the bed until we got up. Finally Anna felt the bouncing. We both had been made semiconscious from a carbon monoxide leak. The insidious gas had entered through our air conditioning system and filled the entire house and ductwork. Scooby had to work hard to wake us.

We became aware that the smoke and carbon monoxide alarms were going off. Black, thick smoke made it impossible to see anything. We were so afraid. We could hardly find our way out of our master bedroom at the back of the house. By the time we made it to the hallway, the hot carpet burned our bare feet, and we could hardly walk.

Neman ran to the front of the house to open the door. We couldn't tell the source of the fire. Would our house blow up any minute? Where were the cats? We heard them howling and crying but could not find them. Anna dropped down to the floor to crawl out of the house. She called for Schitz and Baby Jerry, who was Zen's new kitten.

We were terrified but still in disbelief. The smoke was too thick down on the floor, so Anna jumped to her feet. She ran toward the front door, while Neman called out, trying to find her. The huge, crackling flames immersed the house in fire. We found the front door and staggered out. Scooby stayed close behind us the whole time.

Neman ran back to the house, burning his hand as he tried to hold the door open for the cats to escape. We believed that Schitz, then thirteen years old, and Baby Jerry were still in the house.

The Losses

After the fire department put the flames out, we were able to walk inside. We found Schitz near the front door. Although he had died by the time the rescuers had entered our home, a thoughtful fireman had moved our dear cat away from the flames. We thank God that Schitz had not burned, but the smoke inhalation had been too much for him. We looked all over for Baby Jerry but could not find him. We prayed that he might have run out of the house when he heard the alarms. Anna left food on the front porch in hopes that the kitten would come home.

Two days later, when we looked around the remains of our house, Scooby started sniffing at our water bed. He kept pacing back and forth. We didn't want to look, but Scooby insisted on drawing our attention to the bed. We moved some of the soaked blankets out of his way and saw Baby Jerry's tail and back legs. Scooby had found the kitten behind the bed. He, too, had not burned, but smoke had overtaken his tiny lungs.

Anna, Neman, Zen, and Scooby-Doo

The fireman medic told us later that, usually when people wake up to a fire with that much smoke in the house, they inhale a first breath, lie back down, and fall asleep. God blessed us with Scooby's persistence and courage. We are still not sure how his lungs avoided filling up with carbon monoxide.

We were only able to retrieve photos on our smoky, black computer hard drive, our wedding certificate, and a few wedding mementos. Twenty-five percent of our clothing was salvaged, because family and friends helped us bag up clothes, and then took them to their homes for washing. Most of our belongings were gone, but it was all just stuff except for our dear cats. Everything else we lost in the fire can be replaced. Our house was destroyed, but we are so very grateful to God that Zen, Scooby, and we were saved.

We are also thankful to all the people who prayed for and assisted us. The afternoon following the fire, neighbors brought coolers, ice, drinks, snacks, and clothes. They offered their houses for

157

Scooby and us. We stayed in various houses before we could rent a place close to our destroyed home. The local firemen and police periodically drove down our road to check on us and make sure no thieves or vandals had gotten into the wreckage.

The Recovery

We know we are truly lucky to be alive. Schitz and Baby Jerry are irreplaceable, but we were blessed with the next best thing. Two months after the fire, we went to the burned house to get floor jacks to give to another family. As we slowly pulled into the driveway, we saw a little kitten walking up our sidewalk to the house. The coloring of the kitten was remarkably similar to Schitz's and Baby Jerry's, a mixture of black and white fur in the same places on the kitty's body with almost identical markings. We posted a notice about this lost kitten around the neighborhood and took him to the veterinarian to see if he belonged to anyone. No one ever claimed him, so we named the kitty Raz. The kitten needed someone to love him, and we were a grieving family that needed a kitten.

Scooby-Doo especially took to having a new kitty companion. When we introduced them to each other, our huge dog wagged his tail and put his head down in submission to the tiny kitten. He brought over a stuffed animal and laid it in front of Raz, as if to say, "I want to be your friend." Once again, Scooby had agreed with our decision to bring a new addition into the family.

The trauma of the fire and our losses has put Scooby in a constant state of protectiveness toward our family. We are working with very knowledgeable people to help him recover emotionally. Scooby attended obedience school to help him overcome his fear of people and certain situations that increase his anxiety. By introducing him to strangers and friends with treats at the ready, he is learning that he doesn't have to constantly react to protect his family. After his heroism in saving us from the fire, he needed to settle down from the tendency to be overvigilant. He's gradually returning to being the laid-back dog who enjoys himself. We pray that Scooby can soon heal and find the comfort he deserves.

Skeptics may wonder how God can ever help when things are unbearable and they don't see a way out. We want to tell them that God might send a precious little angel in the form of a dog, cat, bird, or even a butterfly. Scooby-Doo Bates is a constant reminder that angels really do exist.

MEDITATION

Are there qualities, such as protectiveness, that have developed in you or your dog out of your survival needs? Are those characteristics still working in your or the dog's best interest?

The Dog in Wolf's Clothing

Gloria Bullerwell
Warburg, Alberta, Canada

*H*oot owls call, wildflowers abound, and a paradise of birds visits the site of an ancient aboriginal ceremonial ground near the North Saskatchewan River. Deer, moose, wolves, coyotes, and a variety of wildlife roam these acres. At what is now our Buck-a-boo Acres Nature Retreat, Cree and Blackfoot tribes once lived and witnessed ever-changing colors of the northern lights painting the sky. In this place of many spirits, a hundred goats, a human family, and two amazing dogs dwell in harmony.

Far away from cities, we live so close to the animals that we get to know what they are thinking, what they want, and how they may react. The deer come here in the winter. I can almost walk right up to them. I have birds on this ranch and a spoiled little squirrel. I put out sunflower seeds and a mixture of peanuts for the birds. I place the squirrel's food in a dog dish, and the squirrel eats it. One evening I was late with the food. That little squirrel came up and smacked me on the hand. So I purposely refrained from immediately giving her the food, just to see what she would do. She smacked my hand a second time.

Out of all the animals here, the ones that fascinate me most are a mated pair of Maremmas. This is an Italian breed of livestock guardian dogs with two thousand years of genetics that enables them to preserve the integrity of ancient lands.

Most people know little about Maremmas. They aren't meant to be a family or house pet. They don't socialize with humans. Their mission in life is to guard livestock. We don't let anybody into the pen with the Maremmas unless we are around, because the dogs might mistake them for predators. Even our house dogs aren't allowed to get too close to the pen where the Maremmas live with the goats.

The dogs' guarding traits don't adapt well for human needs. If Maremmas are around small children, they become overly protective. I knew of a woman who mistakenly thought a Maremma would be a good pet for her husband. He had a business as a mechanic, and the dog wouldn't let his customers (predators) onto the lot. The dog had been placed into the wrong situation and acted instinctively. It is necessary to let these dogs do what they do best, protect the livestock.

Maremmas are born in the pen and live with the livestock they guard throughout their lives. The livestock sleep and curl up with the dogs. Baby goats jump all over and play on them. The Maremmas are constantly on guard, but since most predators roam at night, that is when the dogs go to work protecting the herd. The mother Maremmas begin training their pups when the babies start staggering around. By the time the pups are only a couple of months old, they go out with adult dogs to learn how to do the jobs at which a Maremma excels.

If a predator decides to come into a pen, the male Maremma

immediately jumps into action and faces him down. If the predator doesn't leave, the male dog takes a step toward him. If the invader takes one more step toward the dog, it will be killed. The female Maremma's job is to gather all the livestock together. She keeps a watchful eye on them until danger has passed and the male has chased away the enemy. If the male needs help, the female assists him. After the goats learn to trust the dogs to do a good job, they no longer panic.

Our First Maremmas

After my husband, Dave, and I moved way out to the sticks of Alberta, Canada, to raise livestock and start our ecotourism guest ranch, we needed a dog to protect our goats. Our first Maremma was a five-month-old female named Bouncer. Bouncer is white, as are all pure Maremmas. Her body type is short, very stocky, and muscular with a dense undercoat for winter and a medium-long, wavy topcoat. She has short, floppy ears, close to the head, and a bushy tail. Bouncer is about the height of a German shepherd. Like a bouncer in a bar, she was supposed to get rid of the troublemakers.

The first night we were here, coyotes came to menace the goats on our ranch. Bouncer was still a puppy and didn't have the strength that a mature dog would have to fight them off. The coyotes knew that she was only a puppy by her bark and whatever other instincts told them that Bouncer would be defenseless against them. Throughout the night, I sat at one end of the corral, and my husband sat at the other end to fend them off. I said, "We need another dog."

The next day, we found a two-year-old dog who was already working at another ranch. We had to drive a distance to pick him up and bring him home with us. His name was Icy, because in the winter when the ice was broken in the water trough, he would grab a piece of ice and start chewing on it. Icy is much taller than Bouncer, a big boy, about the height of a Shetland pony. He is very muscular but not as stocky as Bouncer.

Usually a goat picks a dog with whom to have a special relationship. The goat and dog curl up together and bond. But all my goats were immediately fond of Icy and slept near him in the barn.

Before long, Icy trained the younger Bouncer in the duties of a female guardian dog. To watch Icy teach Bouncer what to do and when to do it was a sight to behold. There was absolutely no need for instructions from a human. If a predator approached, it was Icy's

Gloria's Icy and Bouncer

job to move to the fence and bark. He made Bouncer stay back from the fence to go and watch the herd. Then Bouncer checked every shelter where the goats might be until she knew the locations of each of them.

Maremmas never put their teeth on the livestock when rounding them up. Bouncer is always firm but gentle with her goats. After she had her first litter of pups, if there was danger from a predator, she tucked her own pups into the herd of goats. When threatened, Bouncer gathers the goats and makes them stay together so she can keep an eye on them. No matter how big the herd might be, she can tell if a goat is not there. If even one goat is gone, Bouncer can find him. We swear she can count.

One time, Bouncer herded the goats, but a mother goat went looking for her missing baby. Bouncer knew that the babies were all safely in the barn. She pushed the doe from the end of the corral and away from the fence, where Icy was chasing off a big pack of coyotes. After the danger had passed, Bouncer went to every shelter and counted the goats. All were safe, and mom and babies reunited.

Bouncer and Icy Have Babies

It was a happy day for all of us, and especially Icy, when Bouncer had her first litter of puppies. My girlfriend Mavis, whom the dogs know, and I went into the pen after the babies were born. Icy grabbed Mavis's hand and walked her over to the puppies. The proud papa was obviously showing off his new family, who looked like tiny polar bears.

We built a shelter for Bouncer and the pups. When they were only a month old, she started moving them into the main barn. I'd move them back out of the barn, because I was afraid a goat might accidentally step on a puppy. Every time I turned around, Bouncer had returned the pups to the barn.

One night I saw that Bouncer had left the puppies in a corner of the barn while she and Icy were out working. I came back to find a group of yearling does circled around the babies. They were making sure that no one stepped on the pups. I realized then that the goats would always look out for the puppies while the Maremmas were working.

Icy Improvises

Although I had researched and therefore knew a lot about what Maremmas are bred to do, I still had a shock over something Icy did one night. It seemed to call for a more creative imagination and better problem-solving skills than could be explained by his instinct alone.

I was in the house and thought I heard a wolf howling. The next night, I heard the wolf howling again. This time, I went out to look. I knew that when a predator comes around, there's an invisible line Icy has drawn. If a predator crosses that line, he starts barking. If the predator doesn't leave, Icy's barking becomes more insistent.

That night, I was surprised to find that a large pack of coyotes had come close to the fence. They stood their ground and seemed to taunt Icy. Those coyotes were unfazed by the sound of Icy's loud and persistent barking. About the only thing coyotes fear are their natural predators, the wolves.

As I took in this scene, I again heard the sound of a wolf's howl. Then I realized that it was coming from Icy. I had never heard him howl like a wolf. I had never heard of any Maremma howling like a wolf. But Icy figured out how to scare the coyotes away by making the sound of the one predator they fear. I was absolutely astounded by this. At the sound of the wolf's howls, the coyotes were gone in an instant. It turns out that one of Icy's male pups has inherited this talent or been taught by his dad how to howl like a wolf when there is danger from the coyotes.

Icy is getting older now. I'll keep one of the babies from his last litter with Bouncer, who has now been spayed. Maremmas don't live as long as house dogs. Their domain is the outdoors. Their mission is to guard the herd. Although they show love and loyalty to humans, the livestock are their family. We can always count on the Maremmas to keep our goats safe, even if Icy has to pretend to be a wolf. These dogs truly are guardian angels. Just ask our livestock.

MEDITATION

How has a dog shown you that his or her service extends to giving to and caring for all life?

CHAPTER FIVE

A Mission to Teach

Do dogs really have a conscious and rational mind that works like our own? Another way of stating this question is: Is the anthropomorphic assumption correct? The simple answer is that at some level it must be correct or we would have abandoned it long ago as being a useless habit of thought. In our usual interactions with dogs, we normally treat them as if they had at least some lower level of consciousness.

— Stanley Coren

I'm a Zoom Kid

Deb Richeson
Smithfield, Kentucky

*C*an one dog change the course of a person's life? The answer is yes. But Zoom, my focused little dog, changed the lives of students and teachers in an entire school. First, he managed to rearrange my chosen priorities.

Showing dogs competitively used to be my passion, and achieving my business goals was my main pursuit. Paying attention to my family came in at a distant third. I had a demanding corporate job that I'd worked all my adult life, clawing my way to the top of a Fortune 500 company. I never turned down assignments. I stayed late and spent weekends at the office. My family suffered from my inattention, but I didn't see any of that.

On the other hand, my work brought a very nice salary that allowed us to take wonderful family vacations. My daughter loved the many scuba diving trips to the Gulf Coast. We could buy luxury items for my family and both sets of parents. My daughter attended private school, took music lessons at the local university, had a trendy wardrobe, a college account, and a car. We saved enough to purchase our dream acreage in the country. Having money also allowed my daughter and me to travel the countryside to attend dog shows and sample local cuisines, do educational siteseeing, and meet new, wonderful people.

Then my hectic existence fell apart. The events that toppled me clustered into a yearlong period. They made me rethink what my life was really all about.

Life Happens

Our daughter became pregnant in high school. We found out the night she graduated. She started college that fall but then got involved in drugs, which goes against everything my husband and I believe in. Life was a horrible emotional roller-coaster as we struggled to get her back on track. After our daughter had her baby, she left our grandson to live with us.

It was an eye-opening experience to go through the legal system and deal with a dual-addicted family member who disappeared for days and weeks at a time. The family-court judge suggested that we adopt our grandson, and we did. Right after all of that, my brother-in-law, Kenny, whom I loved like a brother, was diagnosed with terminal brain cancer. I sat with him in a hospice facility for the last two weeks before he died.

After Kenny's death, the kennel partner with whom I had shown dogs for twenty years, gave me Zoom, a young Cardigan Welsh corgi, to raise and train for the show ring. I didn't know it at the time, but Zoom would live up to his name. His mission was to move me quickly from my previously selfish ways into the joy and fulfillment of giving service.

Zoom Enters

Right away, I noticed that Zoom's temperament was different from all the other Cardigans I'd known. He was a bombproof dog who never startled or showed fearfulness. He was very calm and loving. I called him my Velcro dog, because wherever I went, he went. He was exceptionally trusting and knew that I would never take him into a situation where he'd be hurt. He had a regal manner and a great deal of self-assurance.

Zoom grew to become a large, powerful dog with the short, little legs of his breed, which allowed the dogs to herd cattle and dodge from underneath hooves when the cows kicked. Zoom has a long body but heavy bone mass. His brushy tail is like a fox's, except it touches the ground. He has a well-chiseled face with black around his eye area and big, tan patches on both cheeks. His white muzzle protrudes from the top of his skull. His large ears stand upright, making him appear constantly alert. He has black body fur and four white paws with a white tip at the end of his tail. He weighs forty-four pounds.

Even though Zoom was beautifully proportioned, his show-dog career was fast and short lived. We never looked back with regret after we stopped taking him to dog shows. In my new way of looking at things, I realized that, for this stage of my life, showing dogs had become a shallow way of spending my time and energy.

Zoom Becomes a Therapy Dog

I started basic obedience training with Zoom, teaching him to sit, stay, lie down, and walk off-lead. In what seemed a very natural progression, I gravitated toward preparing him for certification by Therapy Dogs International. This seemed to be a good fit for his mellow personality.

We left our home in Louisville, Kentucky, and bought acreage in a rural area of Henry County, where we built our little homestead. When we had adopted my grandson, I made a commitment that if God gave me a second chance, I would not fail my family this time by being too busy and wrapped up in my work. Consequently my grandson became, and still is, the center of my life's focus.

Deb's Zoom

After I got Zoom certified as a therapy dog, for about a year, he visited with hospice patients at a local nursing home. The volunteer work was satisfying for him and me. Around that time, I started to get familiar with staff at New Castle Elementary School in Henry County, which my grandson attended. I found out that a disproportionate number of children at this school were not able to read at grade level. These children didn't like or want to read.

At the end of my grandson's school year, I went to the award program. I watched the children get academic awards and recognition for art pieces and other things but not for reading.

The at-risk kids who weren't reading well had had intervention and attended special needs classes. Many of them put forth effort to learn. The reading resource and Title I teacher, Mary Roberts, struggled to help them improve. In spite of her efforts, the children needed to make more progress.

I wasn't as involved in my daughter's school life as I should have been. Now that we lived in this rural community, I wanted to participate more in the school my grandson attended. So I began volunteering at the school and learned that they were making a push for literacy. I approached the principal, Barbara James, about bringing in a therapy dog. I said, "The elderly people love Zoom. Isn't there something Zoom and I could do at school?"

Even though Barbara had never heard of therapy dogs, she was open-minded. She said, "Sure, bring your dog in here." Soon Mary Roberts implemented the Tell-a-Tail program to complement the school's literacy efforts. From one of Zoom's visits until their next session, the children could practice reading the books that Mary had assigned.

None of us could have guessed that having Zoom come to school would turn into such a roaring success. We were soon to discover that the school's literacy initiative, Zoom, and I made a strong team.

Zoom Goes to School

Zoom became the bright spot in the children's school day. He is essentially the school dog. He has helped the at-risk students become excited about reading. One of the children commented that Zoom's big ears must have been made for listening because he does it so well. While a child reads to Zoom, if the youngster needs assistance, I sound out the words and give clues. After the reader finishes, I check comprehension by asking questions.

One of Zoom's first special needs children was a third grader named Caroline. A selective mute, Caroline was only mildly mentally challenged and had the ability to communicate verbally, but she chose not to speak. The teachers couldn't figure out whether or not Caroline could read, because she didn't test well enough to get an accurate score. After evaluating her, a child psychologist from the Kentucky health program informed the school that Caroline probably could not be educated. However, the staff at our school never gave up on her.

Kim Moody, Caroline's third-grade special education teacher, asked if Zoom could come in and sit with Caroline for a couple of hours a week. So we arrived for our first visit, with Zoom's big dog pillow in tow.

Caroline was in the room with three other students, yet Zoom went directly to her. He did this the first visit and every other time he came to that room. He was so bonded to Caroline from day one that it sometimes caused a bit of hurt feelings among the other children.

Always keeping her hair pulled around to cover her face like a curtain, Caroline would look at the floor, as if she were uninterested in anything going on around her. But when Zoom cuddled near her on his pillow, she made eye contact with him.

I asked Caroline if she would like to read a book to Zoom. I said, "Zoom has his own book in his suitcase."

I opened Zoom's suitcase and took out one of the books the reading resource teacher had supplied. Mary's book selections are specifically geared to the levels and interests of the students. I handed the book to Caroline. She started reading it with her mouth moving and silently forming words.

I said, "Zoom loves to hear children read. He never makes fun of kids."

Caroline read this book out loud. Watching Caroline read aloud for the first time, Kim burst into tears. The students jumped out of their chairs and began clapping. They shouted, "Look, Caroline is reading. We knew she could read!"

After Caroline finished reading to Zoom, she threw her shoulders back and walked proudly into the hall. In only one session, Caroline had become a Zoom Kid.

Her parents did not believe what had happened with Caroline and Zoom. Kim invited them to school, and they came in to listen to their daughter read. It was wonderful to see how surprised and happy they were for this child who rarely spoke. They had proof that Caroline had crossed the bridge to literacy.

Three years later, I went with Zoom to the Cardigan Welsh corgi national dog show, which was held in Kentucky. The dog show invited the special needs children from New Castle Elementary School to be the guests of honor and walk with Zoom around the show ring along with their teacher Kim Moody. When these kids walked into the dog show with Zoom, it was a great cultural experience for them.

Caroline stole the show. After experiencing Zoom's doggy therapy sessions, Caroline spoke freely and without trepidation. She had written an essay about what Zoom meant to her. She read it to the crowd of over four hundred strangers.

Special needs students have individual education plans designed by the teachers to give them what they need to succeed in school. The teachers made Zoom an essential component of Caroline's individual education plan.

Before Caroline graduated to middle school, the special needs teachers there asked me if Zoom could accompany Caroline for a tour. Caroline and Zoom would take a walk through the middle school to orient her to the new environment so that she would not be overwhelmed on the first day. I handed her Zoom's leash and let Caroline lead him through the tour. By the time they finished, Caroline was ready to take on middle school.

The Zoom Reward System

At New Castle Elementary School, reward often consists of playtime with Zoom. If a child acts inappropriately in class, the teacher might say, "You will not be able to see Zoom this week." This settles down any disruptive behavior in a flash.

A second-grade boy has compliance disorder. This means that he acts out on his frustrations. Zoom has become his carrot. If the boy erupts in his regular classroom, he goes to the special needs class. The reward for reining in his behavior is playtime with Zoom. When he regains control of himself, he can sit in the room and read to Zoom. If the weather is nice, he can walk Zoom around the school property.

Zoom Kids receive rewards after each reading session. They get to choose from little policeman badges, a dog show rosette, and other small toys. Each child has his or her picture on a sheet of paper with the caption, "Zoom said I was a great reader today. I got to read to Zoom today."

There is no teacher's lounge in this small, rural school, so teachers have go to the principal's office for emotional meltdowns. Even they take mental-health breaks with Zoom. Periodically I hear our names called out over the school intercom system, either for a teacher or a child who is having a tough time. We hurry to the principal's office for Zoom to work his charming magic on the person, relaxing away their worries and stress.

Zoom's Day at School

Zoom loves the days when he goes to school. I can see a difference in him when he is off or on duty. On school days he goes into a more alert mode. He stays very attentive at the school. At home he's a typical dog who simply likes to spend the day sleeping and playing.

Zoom recognizes the routine on school days. He sees me in the bathroom, fixing my hair and putting on clean clothes. He watches me with a great deal of focus. To prepare for school he wears a special collar that has his Therapy Dogs International and rabies tags on it. Usually he's very laid-back, but when he hears those tags rattle, he gets frantic and starts jumping straight up in the air, whining, dancing, and barking.

I get his suitcase, and he runs out to our van, waiting impatiently for me to open the door. He bolts to his seat and lies down during the drive. When the car turns into the school parking lot, he looks out the window and whines with excitement. He strains to get into the reading-resource room door as we walk through the parking lot. At lunch, he takes a potty break outside. Then he watches me eat with the staff. Afterward, it's time for him to go to the special education room.

Zoom has a three-by-five-foot dog pillow that is hunter green and embroidered on the corner. On it is a cartoon dog with a big, happy smile on his face and a circle around him that says, "Zoom's Reading Pad." The pillow goes with us from room to room. The children can sit with Zoom, lie on their tummies, or take whatever position is most comfortable for them.

Zoom's suitcase is bright blue carry-on luggage with wheels and a retractable handle. In it we keep Zoom's and the children's snacks and Zoom's water bowl. We carry books Mary has selected for the children to read to Zoom. She tries to find animal-themed books, because the children respond much better to them.

His school schedule is rigorous for a dog. He doesn't get many naps during the day, because we visit with as many kids as possible without overtaxing him. So far, he hasn't shown any signs of burnout, even though we average five hours a day, three days per week, with the children. That is a lot of work for one dog.

If no children are in the reading room, Zoom goes in the corner and takes a doggy power snooze until the next group arrives.

I've noticed that when Zoom has an emotionally charged session with a child who is upset for some reason, he shows signs of being stressed. He starts to yawn, and his eyes wander. I take him into the principal's office and let her know that Zoom needs quiet time. Barbara leaves her office and closes the door behind her. Zoom crawls underneath her desk and takes a nap.

Zoom Kids Succeed

There is empirical evidence of the benefits of having therapy dogs in our school. Each year we see the at-risk children's reading test scores rise. This has been our best year ever.

Barbara wrote an article about how Zoom helped to raise the school's reading scores, and it was published in the *Kentucky Teacher* newsletter. Our local newspaper did a front-page story on Zoom. Then the *Courier-Journal* and *Fox 41 News* in Louisville picked up the story. They filmed Zoom interacting with the reading students. *USA Today* published a little blurb about how Zoom helped to raise the children's reading scores. *Newsweek* mentioned in an article on dogs helping children to read that the therapy dog at our rural school was helping kids to be more successful.

When the Zoom story hit the *Kentucky Teacher* newsletter, the school was inundated with phone calls and emails. People wanted to know how we got the results and what they could do to get dogs into their schools. Mary and Barbara forward most of these types of messages to me so I can respond in an effort to help people locate a local therapy-dog team.

Mary Roberts received emails from a young Minnesota man who was working on his master's degree and asked for specifics about the Zoom program. He wanted to bring dogs into the inner-city school to help at-risk readers. I believe this program is needed across the country. Unfortunately, the demand for therapy dogs is greater than the current supply.

The children say to me, "I hope I'm a Zoom Kid next year. I won't read this summer, and I might forget everything I've learned, so I need to be a Zoom Kid next year too." They do not want out of the Tell-a-Tail program.

The special needs students started a scrapbook to keep mementos of their visits with Zoom. They are required to submit portfolios at the end of each school year that contain samples of their writing. They can write about any subject. Starting with the first year Zoom came to read with them, all the students wrote animal-related stories for their portfolios. They feel good about their positive experiences with an animal.

The New Castle Elementary School awards students with a certificate and badge, signed by Zoom, when they achieve their reading goals. Now our special needs children are getting these awards. I've watched tears flowing from parents as their children received certificates for reading achievement.

I don't know if being a Zoom Kid will change the children's lives permanently and give them what they need to be successful adults.

But one thing I do know is that they will walk away from this school knowing that a dog cares and will never judge or correct them. Zoom loves them unconditionally.

Zoom accompanies me to the post office, shopping, and school. He is not denied access anywhere in this little rural community. Everyone knows him. I've started seeing signs that Zoom is having a long-term effect on the at-risk students.

Going to Wal-Mart is quite an experience, because it takes me longer than most people to get around the store. When we meet former Zoom Kids who have gone on to middle school, they first ask, "Where is Zoom?" Then they say things like, "Tell Zoom I am still reading, but I'm not in the special reading program anymore." They want me to tell Zoom what book they are reading currently or which books they especially like to read.

When I return home, I always follow through by telling Zoom what the children said and giving him their regards.

I had to be absent for an entire month when I needed emergency knee surgery. Everyone at school was disappointed not to see Zoom for so long. The special needs children were devastated. Then Kim had the idea of having the children send photos of themselves to Zoom and email their questions to him. A new project emerged in which the children could do their homework with Zoom over the Internet.

I asked Kim, "How are the kids handling Zoom's being away?" I offered to send pictures and a note from Zoom. The children were ecstatic. Kim said the children benefited from learning new technology and how to form questions to ask Zoom.

Zoom Kids Get Emotional Support

One of the Zoom Kids is severely autistic. We don't work with her regularly because we're afraid of injury, since she tends to get too physical and extremely agitated. When we let her pet Zoom, the teacher guides the child's hand down his back in a slow, repetitive motion. She feels his soft, firm body and warmth. Zoom lies there, rock still, which calms the child.

In another instance where Zoom gave emotional support, a boy came to school one day looking exceptionally unsanitary. We were aware that his home life was tragic beyond words. He had some physical deformities and signs of abuse on his body. He was very upset that day, and the teacher called me to his room.

I let the boy crawl up on the pillow with Zoom. I sat quietly nearby to make sure nothing happened that might cause the dog harm. The child wrapped his little arms around Zoom's neck and started whispering in his ears. Tears rolled down the child's cheeks. He told Zoom why he was having a bad day. His parents had made him sleep in the barn with all the barn cats, and he was so hungry. When the boy finished confiding in him, Zoom turned around and licked his little face.

It's tragic that a child has such experiences, but then it's a godsend that he had one little dog to reach out to for comfort. The teachers, guidance counselor, and social services staff did what they could for this boy, but they were adult authority figures. Just that this warm, furry dog gave him a big kiss let the child know that it would be okay. I wish there could be therapy dogs in every school to heal the children's wounds.

When Zoom looks at me, he communicates trust, devotion, and love. He is my port in the storm and does therapy work for me too. After I see and hear some horrible things these children endure, I need my therapy session with Zoom at home.

My nine-year-old grandson says hi to Zoom when he sees him in the hallways at school. He's proud that his family dog is in the school helping kids. He's a bit of a geek, and Zoom gives him bragging rights. Sports dominate here, and my grandson is not one of the popular, sporty kids. But he gets to walk Zoom out of school. He's also helping me train Jozette, a second Cardigan Welsh corgi, who will take the Therapy Dogs International test and serve as Zoom's backup.

Through education, children can break out of the generational cycle of ignorance and poverty, and have a fuller, happier, and more rewarding life. Realistically I know that one person and one dog, even Zoom, can't save them all, but saving one child is a start. What if every willing and able adult could save just one child through an hour or two of volunteer time weekly at their local schools? The possibilities are so exciting.

I'd never go back to working in the corporate world. I've had my second chance; I want to focus on my family and what matters most in life. The truth of the matter is, I'm a Zoom Kid too.

MEDITATION

What special skills and interests do you have that would foster and support a relationship between dogs and schoolchildren in your home or community?

My Dog-Training Partner Is a Dog

Heather Mitty
Golden Valley, Minnesota

*W*atching my husband, Mike, roll into the parking lot of our building, I saw the expression of happiness on his face. I would've loved to have shared in his delight, but I wasn't so sure about welcoming the all-black bundle that Mike carried from the car. It seemed to be made of only ears and legs. Mike had just returned from a trip to visit his mother. To everyone's surprise, he had announced that a sixteen-week-old German shepherd puppy would be coming home with him.

Mike had fallen in love with the puppy's big, brown eyes and her sad facial expression. On the phone a few days earlier, he had pleaded his case. He promised to walk the dog, take her for training, and work with her. I would never have to lift a finger.

Though immediately excited about the prospect of having a puppy chosen by my husband, I also felt concerned. Mike and I had just gotten our first place together, and the apartments didn't accept dogs over fifty pounds. This dog could grow up to be at least that weight.

We already had a dog to walk in Minnesota's frigidly cold winters, and we didn't always agree about who would take on that chore. What would happen if we had two dogs who needed to go outdoors several times daily?

We Already Had a Perfect Dog

In my opinion we already had the perfect dog, our golden retriever, Carmen. She and I had bonded to the extent that we had one of those mind-reading dog-person relationships. She was my first puppy, and to this day she only has eyes for me. Mike often watched Carmen and me play together and commented that we loved each other more than anyone else on earth. In arguing his case for bringing home the puppy, he persisted with the point that he wanted a puppy of his own. I, too, hoped he would have the kind of relationship with a dog that I had with Carmen.

In addition to not relishing the idea of having another dog, I had a lot of preconceived notions about German shepherds. I was sure that the dog would be scary and ugly, and there would be nothing puppylike about her. I pictured German shepherds as aloof and not at all like a cuddly and warm dog who would hang on my every move. The look of the adult German shepherds worried me. I had always perceived them as unpredictable dogs, and their quick, silent movements unnerved me.

Perhaps as a way of luring me into the idea of adopting the puppy, Mike told me I could name her. I decided to take him up on the offer and selected the name Lola, because it sounded exotic and regal. Later, when I found out that the name Lola has German origins, I was quite proud of myself for having thought of it for our new German shepherd.

Upon seeing Lola that first day, when she bounded out of our car with Mike, I will be honest and say that my heart sank. To me, a puppy is soft and fluffy with sweet features and a cuddly little body. At sixteen weeks, Lola was long and skinny. Her ears were remarkably oversized, taking up her entire head. I didn't think she could ever grow into them and figured they would always be too big.

An Imperfect Dog

In those first days with us, this puppy was awkward and timid, and would not stop crying. The only one who could comfort her worried heart was Carmen. Immediately Lola was convinced that Carmen controlled the sun and the moon, but Carmen had no special affection for the new intruder to her peaceful home.

Lola's first weeks with us were filled with stress, confusion, and fear. It is a wonder that any of us survived. When German shepherds are left alone, being very sensitive, they are prone to anxiety and getting into trouble. It soon became obvious that Lola hadn't had the proper socialization experiences she needed before coming to live with us. She simply did not understand much of the world and seemed overwhelmed at every turn.

My dear husband was quickly in over his head. He wanted so badly to comfort the little ball of sadness. I knew from training Carmen that it is counterproductive to baby an upset puppy or get too overprotective. It teaches them

Heather's Lola

to rely too heavily on human support. Even though Mike had had the best of intentions in becoming Lola's primary person, he needed to slowly start giving up the reins. He left Lola's training up to me, because I had successfully settled Carmen into our home.

We wound up spending hundreds of dollars for behaviorists, medications, crates, and toys for Lola. We fretted over what to do with this large, nervous puppy. She never tried to cuddle. She didn't want to be held and wouldn't listen to our requests. If we left her at home alone with Carmen, Lola would have an emotional meltdown. The neighbors reported that they heard her barking for hours each day while we were away at our jobs. She was often so frazzled that she messed in her crate. Each night, we came home to a dirty and upset puppy.

Slowly we worked through each of Lola's behavioral issues. We attended every doggy training class we could find. I spent a lot of time trying to help this little furry baby who seemed to need me so much.

My daily attempts to train Lola humbled me in my understanding of the dog world. While Carmen was the kind of dog who would lie on my feet, Lola always found a spot in the corner to lie down, away from human contact. At the dog park, Carmen would bolt ahead out of sight, but insecure Lola ran ahead a little and then stopped, came back, and checked to make sure I was still there. Lola did not care about food. We soon learned that she was motivated by praise. But too much positive attention scared her and shut her down.

After about six months of persistent care and training, Lola finally seemed to be ready to blossom. At ten months old, she approached me to be petted for the very first time. It was so amazing. She had finally decided to trust us. She increased her affection and attention a little bit every day. As she matured, we were treated to Lola's nuzzling our hands, sticking her big nose in our faces, and sometimes even planting a kiss on our cheeks. Although she never enjoyed wrestling with humans, she appreciated gentle play.

Lola Gets a Job

As Lola reached adulthood, it occurred to me that she might benefit from having a job. I am extremely guilty of treating my dogs like my children and constantly try to think of new ways to make their lives more fulfilled. Through my research on herding breeds, I knew that German shepherds thrive through work. I also learned that mental stimulation is beneficial to dogs and can make them calmer. I noticed that Lola would light up at watching children play at the park. So at first, I thought we could volunteer and find a way for her to work with children.

Lola had completed several levels of obedience training by then, and I was very happy with her progress. She excelled at skills that Carmen — bless her — will never be good at. Lola always came back when I called her. She never left heel position when we were out walking, and she became very focused while we worked together. I decided to work toward a therapy-dog certification for Lola and looked forward to giving her this type of challenging opportunity.

Unfortunately, a horrible accident in the backyard left Lola with a broken leg just as we were set to launch her onto a new career path. Right before Christmastime, she was running up the stairs on the deck and slipped on an icy patch. This injury was a scary ordeal that reminded Mike and me of the depth of our love for our creatures. Mike cared for Lola night and day. Through dozens of vet appointments and all the medication, he was always by her side when she needed something. Due to her long healing process, we were far from achieving the goal of having Lola become a certified therapy dog.

While Mike and I struggled to help Lola recover and find a job, I began thinking about the kind of work I was doing, too. As a mortgage broker, I worked long hours with stressful responsibilities that weren't offset by how well the job paid. Mike and I had overcome so much with Lola that I thought my personal experiences could help me relate to others who cry, curse, and worry about their own pets. The idea of being a dog trainer appealed to me. I believed that I could be good at it because of all the experience I had gained from the trainers who had taught us how to deal with Lola. I also had a great deal of empathy for the woes of people who are overwhelmed by their dogs.

In the past I had felt such profound guilt over the lack of time we spent enjoying our pets each day. Our busy lives were very hard on them. Dogs need their people. The amazing perk of being a dog trainer would be more time spent with Lola and Carmen. I knew I'd control my hours, work mainly nights and weekends, and possibly be able to involve my dogs in the work. The new schedule as a dog trainer would mean that when I worked, Mike would be at home. This way the dogs would only have to spend three hours a day alone. I looked forward to seeing both of them become much happier girls.

I eventually decided that I had to follow my heart. I closed my eyes, jumped in with both feet, trusted my instincts, and became a full-time dog trainer.

Looking for a Dog-Training Partner

I also began toying with the idea that Lola might turn into my perfect partner for my new dog-trainer job. By going through the difficult months of training her, I had discovered that dogs need to think every day. Lola had grown into a beautiful dog and could best be described as warm, attentive, and loyal. Mike and I both felt proud of how far she had come. When I looked into her deep and thoughtful eyes, I often thought that she understood every word I said and grasped the way things should be with dogs and people. I was realistic enough to know that she would always be a high-strung girl. Her basic personality meant that I would continue to struggle with her quirks. But it occurred to me that, by having a dog-training job and making Lola my assistant, she and I both might be able to find more meaningful and satisfying work.

Lola started going to work with me several days a week as a demonstration dog for my training classes. We worked in a busy pet store with a training area at the center. At first, she seemed stressed with all of the sights and sounds. There were constant distractions with dogs barking or rushing up on her, smells of food, and the scents of other pets. The crowds of people meant that many would thrust their hands around the top of Lola's head to say hello. She particularly disliked that motion and considered it to be rude and intrusive human behavior.

The hardest part for Lola was staying focused when something caught her eye. She constantly scanned the area to check on dogs and people. She tired quickly and found it hard to relax in such a chaotic environment. I learned to read her body language and give her frequent breaks. I made sure we spent a few minutes outside every few hours to take play breaks.

Over time, Lola became desensitized to the distractions and learned the dog-training and pet-store routines. Lola's getting to know my staff helped her become more relaxed. If I thought she needed down time, she went off with a manager for a nap in the store office.

Slowly the two of us got into a rhythm. I found working with Lola to be much like dancing with the same partner for a very long time. We had to learn each other's moves and gain the ability to easily predict what would come next. I could tell when she had shifted from the emotionally difficult adjustment period to a state of anticipation when she started howling in excitement as I loaded her up to go to work with me.

The Amazing Lola, My Canine Co-worker

After Lola mastered the routines of working with me to train other dogs, amazing things started to happen. I noticed that when we walked into the building where we taught classes, she began to emit a sense of calm. She does not have this demeanor at home or when we go out on the town.

At doggy school, my canine co-worker watches over all that goes on but respects the space of every dog and person. She restrains herself from trying to satisfy natural curiosity about objects or living things. She has her moments of frustration and gets tired, but I've never seen Lola lose patience.

Lola has taught me many more lessons than I will ever master. She gives unconditionally. On days when she is asleep in the corner of the ring and clearly exhausted, when I ask for her, she shows up at my side. She is always excited about work, no matter how many hours we have to put in. I sometimes forget that she is nearby, because she waits so patiently and quietly. She is certainly the definition of a reliable co-worker.

Many dogs attending our training classes have a great deal of fear and distrust of other dogs from a lack of previous opportunity to interact with them. Just like people, they are not born knowing how others will treat them. They have to be taught. Some people do not know this and wait too long to expose their pets to socialization. By then, a lot of fear and misunderstanding has emerged. Lola has a peaceful, trust-building presence that calms these worried dogs. The ultimate mother figure, Lola teaches young pups with a look and a small lip movement how to be polite. It is poetic to see her almost-imperceptible movements and the sobering effect they have on young puppies and adolescent dogs with negative attitudes. When dogs need a champion to defend them, Lola steps in to make sure that the other dogs mind their manners in class. She reminds everyone to keep cool if things get a little out of hand.

In my work, there is always a new challenge or someone who needs extra attention. I can trust Lola with anything and know that she will support me when I need her. She sits attentively on the sidelines if I have to deal with a situation.

My respect for Lola and her intelligence has grown since we started this adventure of training dogs together. Daily there are moments when I catch myself welling with pride over how much she has grown and become balanced in every way. Even her ears are now a proportional part of her exceptionally beautiful exterior. I love watching her excitement when we pull into the parking lot where we work. I know in my heart that she also feels pride in her abilities. She isn't perfect, but she tries, and that is all I can ask of her.

At the end of an evening's work, we both head home, where Lola curls up and rests contentedly. Our dog, who once had so many physical and emotional issues to overcome, turned out to be the best partner a dog trainer could ever have.

MEDITATION

Which dogs were your best teaching partners? Has a dog who was a handful at first reminded you that with patience, positive changes are possible?

Kutty and Goldie,
India's First Animal-Assisted-Therapy Dogs

Mrs. Minal Vishal Kavishwar
Pune, Maharashtra, India

*L*ike any new arrival, Kutty alternated between being half-nervous and half-curious on her first day at school. Excited children surrounded her as she slowly walked through the corridor. As soon as she spotted me, she ran in my direction. The difference between how other students might meet old friends at the start of a school year and Kutty's greeting was that hers involved crazy wags of a tail, jumping, and licking. This scared, little four-month-old, fawn-colored Labrador retriever puppy was making her debut as a therapy dog that day in June 2003 at the Dharmaveer Anand Dighe Jidd Special School in Thane, India.

Kutty would grow up to be the first dog in India to be trained as a therapy dog according to international standards and certified by the Delta Society as a Pet Partner. Kutty made it possible for me to win the Delta Society's 2007 Beyond Limits award in the category of Animal-Assisted Therapy Practicing Professionals. She has the distinction of being the first therapy dog from India who was part of a team nominated for the prize. Kutty also became a role model for other therapy dogs with my Animal Angels Foundation in Mumbai and Pune.

Along Kutty's journey in providing constant companionship for mentally challenged children, this beautiful, gentle, and understanding dog has taught me a lot about love and compassion. She has been my co-therapist for creating the new field of animal-assisted therapy in India.

Kutty Goes to Jidd Special School

Five years earlier, I did canine counseling and dog training along with my friend Kshitija Koppal, who was one of the first canine counselors in the country. Mrs. Shyamashree Bhosle, principal of the Jidd Special School, had contacted Kshitija and me because

Minal's Kutty at Anand Dighe Jidd Special School

she wanted a dog to work with the children. Kshitija selected the pup Kutty from Bangalore. Kutty was brought to the school to be trained as a therapy dog. Usually purebred dogs in India are pets or show dogs, so Kutty had a novel purpose from the beginning of her life.

At that time, people in India were not familiar with the concept of animal-assisted therapy. Mrs. Bhosle had seen a documentary on Animal Planet about animals who help people with disabilities. She wanted to have a dog at school who would be a good companion and attraction for the children.

I had completed my master's degree in clinical psychology by that time. Since this school educated mentally challenged children, I believed that a properly trained dog would benefit them emotionally.

I had also seen television documentaries about the service that dogs provide to people with disabilities. In my personal experience I spent most of my childhood with dogs rather than people as my best friends. They helped shape my emotions and personality. So I understood what good friends dogs could be to children. After doing a lot of research in the field of animal-assisted therapy, I started training Kutty in the latest methods.

It was decided initially that Kutty would live in the school because she would be trained there. But for Mrs. Bhosle, it was love at first sight. On Kutty's first day at school, she decided to adopt the dog and take her home. True to her name, which means "the youngest one" in the Tamil language, Kutty became the youngest member of the Bhosle family. Mrs. Bhosle brought Kutty to school every day.

When I introduced Kutty to the children I noticed an immediate change in them. They were thrilled. Their responses were, "A dog in our school!" "When will she come to our class?" "Oh! She is looking at me." "What does she eat?" Some of the mentally challenged children were irritable or cranky at times and refused to go to school. Seeing and interacting with Kutty made them all happy. Even the teachers, who used to get frustrated with the children, and the principal, who had to deal with much stress, started smiling, laughing, and talking gibberish to the dog. Anger, stress, and crying disappeared as Kutty transformed everyone's mood and attitude.

From Playful Puppy to Therapy Dog

As a pup, Kutty was very attentive and eager to learn and work. From the initial days of her training, I took her to the classroom to be among the children. Because the job was emotionally demanding, it was not easy for Kutty to be a therapy dog for about eighty mentally challenged children. At first, she was uncomfortable when too many children gathered around her. Neither she nor I knew exactly how to proceed. But Kutty always showed me the way.

As a puppy, Kutty loved to play in the garden adjoining the school. She used to play roughly, running full speed and jumping up on me. She rolled in the mud, getting all dirty, and could be as naughty as any other pup. Kutty had a game in which she ran away with the ball in her mouth and waited for me to chase her. The moment I drew close, she ran farther. I didn't keep her on a leash during playtime, even if she was resting in the principal's office, which was like her den. She only stayed on her leash during therapy sessions.

Kutty wore a therapy jacket that had a body belt attached to it. The moment I put the jacket on her, she knew that it was time for work. She'd even fetch her leash. I'd say, "Where's your belt, Kutty? Come, we have to go to the classroom." I'd take her out to play first and then to the classrooms. This same robust pup who ran like the wind outdoors became gentle and careful around children. The change in her from playful puppy to therapy dog was striking.

Kutty's Miracles

In spite of my being a psychologist, Kutty surprised me with her ability to reach out to the children and bring about miraculous changes in them. If a child lost balance and Kutty was nearby, she gently stepped aside so the child wouldn't stumble over her. If a child cried, she would go near his face and sniff or lick it. The child would then stop crying, look at Kutty, and smile.

She was extremely patient with kids while playing ball. Some children who had motor problems could not throw the ball properly or took a long time. Kutty never snatched the ball away. One paraplegic girl was immobile from the waist down. She had to crawl in order to move. When Kutty played with her, she patiently waited for the girl to throw the ball and then dropped it right in front of the child. Kutty instinctively knew this girl was different from the other children, who didn't need as much care.

Almost all of these things were natural for Kutty to do and nothing that I had taught her. She figured out on her own how to take care of individual children.

Kutty has enriched the lives of many children and adults. There was a child in the Jidd Special School who was paraplegic and mentally challenged. Because he was undergoing physiotherapy, he had been given new leg fittings and crutches to help him walk. He was supposed to take two or three rounds in the school corridor to get used to the apparatuses. So far, he had either refused to exercise or done it begrudgingly. But when we asked the boy to take Kutty for a walk, he was so thrilled that he even made extra rounds.

For Kutty, this was a new activity, and she had to learn what to do to help the boy. As he walked on the crutches, he held Kutty's leash in one hand. Sometimes he pulled on the leash with excitement, and sometimes he staggered or even fell. Kutty remained very observant. She quickly adjusted her pace to the boy's walk. She licked him when he fell, motivating him to do his best. The child is now able to get around with minimal difficulty and is always the first to raise his hand when asked, "Who wants to take Kutty for a walk?"

Another such miraculous story is that of Shahrukh, a mentally challenged boy with associated hearing and speech impairment. Since his admission to the school, Shahrukh had not spoken a single word. Even in the classroom, he remained noninteractive and profoundly nonresponsive. His parents had almost declared him deaf.

After he started interacting with Kutty, everyone was amazed to see Shahrukh become expressive and eager to communicate. It was just that he had not known how to talk with humans. With Kutty, he did not need words. Kutty always seemed to understand what the boy wanted and played with him. She gave him unconditional love and provided a nonjudgmental environment where the boy was not afraid to express himself.

One day, when Kutty ran away with the ball with which they were playing, to everyone's surprise, Shahrukh spoke his first word. He said aloud, "Kutty." Since then, there's been no looking back. Now, with animal therapist Kutty and his human speech therapist to help him, Shahrukh has a lot to say.

Kutty Extends Her Love beyond School

Kutty's selfless service is not limited to the children at the school. When Mrs. Bhosle, Kutty's human mama, was ill with severe heart trouble, Kutty never left her bedside until she recovered. Even though Kutty was only a year-old pup at the time, she showed tremendous maturity at such an early age. Mrs. Bhosle says, "Kutty somehow understood that something was not right with mama and that she should not behave like a pup anymore. It was Kutty's touch and her constant emotional support that helped me go through the toughest time of my life."

Kutty truly proved to be an angel when she worked with the families of the victims of the July 11 Mumbai train blast in 2006. Animal Angels Foundation, along with a team of psychiatrists from King Edward Memorial Hospital in Mumbai, Bombay Psychiatric Society, and the area's Rotary clubs organized a meeting called *Raahat ka Ehsaas*, which means "a sense of relief." There, Kutty comforted the blast-affected families.

This initiative was the first of its kind in India to introduce animal therapy as a medium for rehabilitating post-disaster or post-trauma survivors. An utter professional, Kutty interacted with every person in the room. Before I introduced her, the mood of the meeting had been very grave. The moment Kutty entered, a buzz of excitement and happiness began.

Kutty eased the emotional pain and helped survivors of the blast see the brighter side of life. Kutty turned out to be a big help to many children who had undergone the trauma of losing one or both parents and were not able to express their sorrows. One child hugged Kutty, held her for a long time, and started crying. Now the child has come through her emotional block and moved on with her life.

A Golden-Hearted Dog Named Goldie

Goldie, a three-year-old golden retriever with soft, light-gold fur and perky ears, joined Kutty in the work of animal-assisted therapy around May 2005. For Goldie, life has always been about serving those in emotional distress and giving them a reason to live.

As a pup, Goldie was trained to be an in-house therapy pet for Neil, an autistic child. She was instrumental in bringing about a major change in Neil's expressiveness and vocabulary. Neil kept staring out the window, avoiding interaction with anyone, but he started responding to the tail wags of Spongy, which was the name the family had given Goldie.

Minal's Kutty and Goldie at Anand Dighe Jidd Special School

Neil and Goldie bonded quickly and were soon inseparable. Goldie followed Neil everywhere. Whenever he fixedly stared out the window or at the wall, Goldie moved near him. The dog's touch brought Neil back from his withdrawal.

If Neil started crying or throwing tantrums, Goldie licked the boy's face. Neil then looked at the dog and smiled.

Her bubbly sight provided strong motivation for him to interact with his environment. Her soft, golden fur; wet, compassionate licks; and happily wagging tail gave Neil the excitement and sensory stimulation he needed so desperately. Before long, Neil's happy laughter and Goldie's welcome, playful barks rang through the house.

When Neil's family had to move abroad and couldn't take Goldie with them, she started working as a companion dog for a retired businesswoman, Mrs. Manjiri Chunekar, who was also diabetic and a high-blood-pressure patient. Goldie helped Manjiri de-stress her life and implement a much-needed healthy routine. "She was a wonderful companion, who helped me rediscover the lighter side of my life," says Manjiri.

Goldie is now the pampered pet of the Shrivastava family and caring companion to the two children in the house. Mrs. Shrivastava says that Goldie is just like her third child. Goldie volunteers as a visiting therapy dog in a school for special children, along with volunteers of Animal Angels Foundation. Here, too, she has helped more than a hundred children learn to express themselves and overcome the effects of their disabilities.

Goldie was also a part of the *Raahat ka Ehsaas* program for the emotional rehabilitation of the July 11 Mumbai train-blast victims. She worked with survivors of the blast who had lost their limbs, helping them recover from their pain and loss, and comforting them with her soft hugs.

Kutty and Goldie are two remarkable dogs who have dedicated their lives to improving humans' quality of life. In their career span of almost four years, they have touched thousands of lives. Their mission is to heal mentally and physically ill people, and to spread love and compassion. They have shown that dogs can be much more than simple pets or show dogs. Dogs connect to people in ways that humans can never achieve. They truly are angels.

MEDITATION

How do Kutty and Goldie's examples inspire you to bring hope and joy to those who need to know that they are loved and valued?

CHAPTER SIX

A Mission to Bring Joy and Hope

The animals can do for us, in both the physical and the spiritual orders, what we cannot do for ourselves or for each other. These more precious gifts they provide through their presence and their responsiveness to our inner needs.

— Thomas Berry

Skidboot's Journey

David Hartwig
Quinlan, Texas

*W*hat do Oprah Winfrey, Jay Leno, David Letterman, *Inside Edition*, PAX TV, and Animal Planet have in common? They all celebrated the life and times of Skidboot, my amazing, wonderful, big-hearted blue heeler.

Skidboot was featured on television stations and media outlets all over the world. My wife Barbara and I went along for the ride as Skidboot won the hearts of millions. He demonstrated that, every now and then, God touches somebody or something, creating a special moment. I believe that Skidboot was given to this Texas cowboy to bring joy to people and show that God wants us to smile and enjoy all of creation.

Skidboot came from humble beginnings when he entered our lives on that special Christmas Eve in 1992. A guy named Butch had called for me to come over to his place and trim horses' hooves. This was an unusual request on the day before Christmas, especially since the ranch was thirty to forty miles away, but I said I'd do the job. So I went with my eight-year-old stepson, Russell, on a trip that would change my life forever.

Butch only raised horses, not dogs, but a litter of puppies had taken up residence in his barn. When I asked about them, Butch said that a stray female had started dropping puppies in his yard. He'd picked them up and put them in the barn. I'm sorry to admit that I still hadn't bought a present for Barbara. Knowing how much she loved dogs, I said to Russell, "Let's get your mother one of these puppies and go on home." So we picked the fattest, prettiest pup and put her in my truck.

I grew up in the city, and my dad always had a dog for us, but I didn't consider myself a dog specialist. I had never been to an obedience class or studied dogs. When I was a little boy, the only thing I knew about dogs was that if they didn't come to me when I called, I'd cry. After I moved out to the country, stray dogs showed up at our door, but they didn't become family pets. It was strange for me

David's Skidboot

to want a dog, but I liked the idea of surprising Barbara with the puppy.

After I drove about three or four miles from Butch's place, I looked at Russell, and it was as if something overtook me. I said, "Hey, boy, we didn't think much on picking the puppy. We just took the prettiest one. We didn't check to see if she could hear, if she was cross-eyed or had a cleft palate. We're going to have this dog for a long time. Do you want to go back and see how the other ones act? Maybe pick out a dog who has the right kind of personality for us?"

Even though I didn't want to bother the old-timer, I felt compelled to turn the truck around. In a short time, we were knocking at his door. "Butch, you care if we check these puppies out? Maybe see if we didn't pick the wrong one?" I asked.

"Take them all," Butch said.

Russell and I put the pretty puppy back in the litter. All the puppies were dog-piling, rolling over to show their bellies. One puppy out of the five stood about seven feet from the litter. He acted as if he had something on his mind. I noticed him right off the bat. He was different. I said, "That dog has a smart look." So I grabbed the standoffish puppy, and we went back to the truck to begin the ride home again.

After a while I said, "Russell, we'd better name this dog before Barbara does. If we let her name him, we're going to be stuck with a Precious or a Pumpkin."

Russell said, "Yeah, good idea. What are we going to name him?"

"He's a cow dog. We'll give him a cowboy name."

We started thinking of cowboy-type names: Barbed Wire, Hotshot, and Lariat Rope. All of a sudden the word *skidboot* came to my mind. A skidboot is a leather strap that buckles on top and below, and is worn on the rear fetlock joints of a performance horse. If the horse takes a sliding stop, the skidboot keeps the cowboy from burning the horse's fetlock. Calf ropers are always losing, wearing out, or breaking their skidboots. They're like pads for a baseball player. Skidboot is a common name in the cowboy and rodeo performance world. For some reason, I had no doubt that this was supposed to be the dog's name.

On that cold night I carried Skidboot home zipped inside my jacket. When Barbara saw me holding my hand across my chest, she thought one of Butch's horses must have kicked me. But I opened my jacket and said, "Here's your Christmas present. Take care of him."

Barbara was surprised and happy to receive this last-minute

present. Little did she or I know that the tiny pup would be a gift who kept on giving.

Skidboot Finds His Calling

In the first year of Skidboot's life, I purposely didn't have anything to do with him, because he was Barbara's dog. She proceeded to spoil him. He wouldn't come when we called. He didn't eat unless he wanted to eat. Since Barbara leaves for her job at six or seven in the morning, I'd go outside and have to put up with Skidboot's taking off and running out the door, often to chase the neighbors' chickens.

Skidboot was messing up everything I had. He chewed the burner from my new rope and tore up a new pair of my boots. When he got old enough, he started running after the cows and horses. One of them kicked and broke his leg. A snake bit him, but he survived. If I tried to hold and pet him, he'd chew at my arms. I thought, "That dog must have been bred out of a coyote. There's something wrong with him."

By the time Skidboot was about two years old, I was in my late thirties. I had become real hot at calf roping and performed in rodeos. I wanted to be able to take Skidboot with me on my travels, but he was too wild.

Then one day, I read an article about cow dogs that explained the two types. One kind of cow dog, the border collie and Australian shepherd, herds by going near the cows' heads and leading the livestock to the rancher. The other type of cow dog, the blue heeler, drives livestock away from the rancher's home or barn by nudging the animals' heels.

The article went on to say that if you have a head dog, you can teach him to heel. If you have a heeler dog, good luck because they are hardheaded. If you don't train a heeler dog at a young age to stop when you want him to, that is, "put a whoa on him," there is nothing but trouble ahead for you and the dog.

I realized that Skidboot was a heeler. He would chase and chase. Now he was getting past his youth, and if I didn't start training him to "whoa," there would definitely be trouble ahead.

Training Skidboot Backward

Everybody I ever saw train dogs worked with the dog facing the trainer. If you say, "Sit down," "shake," or "lie down," the dog looks at you. If he doesn't do what you commanded, you help him as he faces you. I thought, if a heeler dog's natural instinct was to have his back to you so he could drive cattle away, why teach him as he faces you? As soon as he turned his back, he wouldn't be in listening mode. He'd be in an "I do what I want to" mode.

I decided that, just for kicks, I'd teach this dog with his back to me. That way, he wouldn't have to face me to understand that he had to do what I said.

As it turned out, it was this one change in the way I worked with Skidboot that made him such an incredibly focused dog. He learned to strictly listen to what I said and didn't rely on body language, hand signals, or treats. Good cow-dog trainers and sheepdog people probably already knew to train a heeler from behind, but it was a new idea for me.

Our first working session involved Skidboot, some dog biscuits, and me. I put my hands down in front of him as he sat between my legs, facing away from me. Every time he tried to get to the biscuit I said, "Whoa," and he ran into my hands. He sat there and stared at the biscuit. Then I said, "Get it," and gave him a little shove from the back. He went off to get the biscuit. I said, "Good. I appreciate that. Now come over. Let's do it again."

Each time, I threw the biscuit farther and blocked him if he started to go for it. After he waited, I let him get it. When he was halfway to the biscuit, I said, "Whoa." He came to a screeching stop and froze, as he had done when my hands had blocked him. In just one short session, he learned how to whoa, because he knew that if he stopped, I'd let him have a reward. After that, we practiced with sticks, toys, and balls.

I enjoy entertaining, so I started thinking up new and unusual tricks for Skidboot and me to do. At the rodeo, somebody would walk by the stable where I kept my horse, and I'd throw a stick out onto the walkway. Then I'd send Skidboot to it. About halfway there, I'd say, "Whoa." He'd go running and then stop in his tracks. People couldn't believe how the dog would freeze. Then I'd say to Skidboot, "You'd better back up." And he'd take a step backward, still staring at the stick. Then I'd say, "Now go get it."

People poked each other and said, "Did you see that?"

Pretty soon, rodeo producers came by to watch Skidboot. This led to my performing with my dog as a rodeo specialty act. By then, I was getting older and it was harder for me to compete profession-ally, so I was glad for the work. A longtime rodeo clown watched Skidboot and me one day and said, "You'll go through ten million dogs and never find one like him. You got yourself a real gold mine."

Most rodeo trick dogs did things like climbing a ladder or jump-ing through a hoop. Skidboot's tricks were unexpected, unusual, and refreshing. He learned to run around a tree in opposite directions until I told him he could get the stick I'd thrown. In a comical routine I called tag-fetch, he'd tag my hand before I'd tell him he could get a toy. Another bit had him imitating my movements by doing things like lifting his paw after I lifted my leg.

Before long, Skidboot and I became celebrities at the specialty rodeos. People flocked to us as we left the arena, wanting to play with Skidboot and asking questions. One person asked, "Is he a real dog?"

At one rodeo a man wanted to talk to me as we walked back to our trailer. He said, "I had a real good dog. He was a grand champion under so many judges in the American Kennel Club." The man started naming off all these clubs he was in.

I said, "Sir, I bet you had a fantastic dog. I got to tell you right now that I'm really not a dog person. I got lucky. I don't know what I'm doing here."

The man smiled at me and said, "That's what I wanted to tell you. It shows that you don't know what you're doing."

"What do you mean?"

"I meant that as a compliment," he said. "You break every good rule of dog training there ever was, and it's just hilarious."

I said, "Thank you. I really appreciate that."

He said, "When you tell that dog to run around the tree before he can get the toy, you're making out as if the dog has cognitive reasoning."

I decided to give him a little sample of cowboy humor. "No sir," I said, "we vaccinate our dogs. They don't have cognitive reasoning or anything like it!"

Memorable Moments with Skidboot

Skidboot was doing so well at entertaining people that I entered Animal Planet's first "Pet Star" contest. Skidboot won the first episode of the program and then came back for the finals. He won the season championship and received a trophy with his name on it, and I got $25,000. That's the largest chunk of money I've ever had at one time in my life. I thought there were much better trained animals in the contest. They had pets who could read, do math, climb ladders, and jump through hoops. But the judges thought Skidboot was the best.

After Animal Planet, our first booking on *The Tonight Show with Jay Leno* allowed Barbara, Skidboot, and me to fly together. *The Tonight Show* called the airline and got celebrity status for the dog. This meant that Skidboot sat on the seat between my wife and me for our trip to the studio in Burbank, California. Barbara gave Skidboot the airplane meal one bite at a time, as if she were feeding a three-year-old child.

We got to ride in a limousine to the NBC studio on the day of the show. It tickled us to see that Skidboot had his own dressing room with his name and star on the door. Inside was a basket with dog and human food. Before the show, Jay visited with us, and we had our picture taken with him.

In the book Ron Westmoreland wrote with me about Skidboot, I told how we rehearsed for *The Tonight Show*. "'I've never seen anything remotely like that dog,' the segment producer said.... 'Do you think we could get him to get out of the limo and walk up to the studio door by himself? That would make a terrific lead-in for the show.'" So Skidboot had a driver open the limo door for him. Then he swaggered over to where I waited for him at the studio door, and his entrance started the show.[1]

When we arrived at the airport each time we were to be guests on a television show, I had our two boarding passes in separate envelopes. I'd say, "Skidboot, you know this routine as well as I do now." I'd hand him the envelope with the boarding pass as we stood in line. He'd wait behind the person in front of him and look around as if he thought, "Come on. Let's go."

Since we always flew with American Airlines, eventually the airline personnel began to recognize Skidboot. The lady who ran tickets through to let passengers board would say, "Hello, Skidboot, is that your ticket?"

He'd hand it to her. She'd run it through and hand it back in the envelope that he carried in his mouth. Then she'd say, "Have a nice flight."

Skidboot would take off down that tunnel to the plane as if he knew where he was going. I'd say, "Would you wait for me?" He'd stop with the ticket in his mouth. I'd say, "You don't know which seat you're in." That didn't seem to matter to him.

Being on *The Oprah Winfrey Show* was probably our media highlight. Everybody said I looked very relaxed, but I was extremely nervous. I believe that if you're passionate about something, it's okay to be nervous. It means that you care. Skidboot performed like a champ on the show. He impressed the audience and Oprah.

We were also on the *Late Show with David Letterman*'s "Stupid Pet Tricks" segment. Other people on the show had their dogs do tricks like running on wheels. These dogs were sniffing, yapping, and barking. I said, "Skidboot, you know better. Let's show some good manners. Sit down and mind your own business."

Early in his career, I taught him not to be a prima donna, and I believe he knew what that word meant. He showed an understanding that it was his duty after each show to be kind and genteel to his fans. They wanted to pet him, shake his paw, and love him. I told him that his job was to show what kindness was all about.

One time as we left a TV show, people who had been at the taping lined up to watch our limousine. As we drove off, they said, "Bye, Skidboot. We love you." I said to Barbara, "They're treating us like celebrity stars." Even though the limo window was open, Skidboot wouldn't stick his head out of it to soak up the adoration. He just knew how to keep fame in perspective.

There were personal moments with Skidboot that I'll always treasure. As I lay in bed after having hip replacement surgery, the visiting nurses came to our home to check on the level of blood thinner I needed to take. Skidboot would lie on my king-size bed and watch the nurses work. I said, "Skidboot, they're taking care of me. They're okay." Sometimes he can be rowdy, but he got very docile because he knew I was recovering.

Another special memory is the night after our performance at a specialty-act showcase for the International Rodeo Association finals. Skidboot and I had to spend the night in the nose of my gooseneck horse trailer in Oklahoma City. The weather was in the single digits. That dog and I huddled up on the mattress together to keep each other warm. It still makes me feel good to think of it.

The Final Act of Skidboot's Show

When he was fourteen and a half years old, Skidboot went blind from macular degeneration. After he was blind, I taught him a new trick. I put his toy on the ground and made a noise with it. He seemed to stare at it, even though he couldn't see it at all.

I said, "Here's the rule: you don't get the toy till I touch your hand." He froze solid and appeared to stare at the toy with his nose right on it. I touched his back, his butt, and his head. As soon as I touched his front paw, which he knows as his "hand," he attacked that toy. Everybody who watched clapped.

I said, "Now, that's not the best part. Let's see if he's really paying attention." Then I said to Skidboot, "This time, here's your toy, but don't get it till I touch your foot." The first thing I did was touch his hand. He didn't get it. I touched his back. When I touched his foot, he finally attacked that toy.

The time finally came when I couldn't travel with Skidboot anymore. We had performed in thirty-eight states, but Skidboot was no longer able to do the things he used to do. In October 2006 I put up a notice on Skidboot's website that said I needed a year to train a new dog in the tradition of Skidboot. I explained that Skidboot had retired.

A while back, *Texas Country Reporter* had done a television piece about Skidboot. After Skidboot's retirement, the video got uploaded to YouTube and other websites. All of a sudden, it sparked a renewed interest in Skidboot all over the world. We got approximately five million hits on the video and a hundred million emails per week. I rebuilt the website and called it "Friends of Skidboot," because I was training Bois d'Arc to carry on Skidboot's legacy. Skidboot's other heirs are our dogs Tie Down and Little Skidboot.

By March 2007, in addition to being blind, Skidboot started having trouble maintaining his weight. His back end went weak, so he had a hard time getting up and down. Often he fell due to spinal cord deterioration. The extent of Skidboot's suffering became clear one weekend when he couldn't eat or drink, hold his head up, or stand.

On Sunday morning, March 25, 2007, I gave Skidboot his last bath out in the yard. The weather wasn't cold, but he started shivering, so I wrapped him in a warm blanket. I took him back into the house and held him to my heart.

That night, Barbara and I said our final good-byes to our old friend as the veterinarian released Skidboot from a body that could no longer serve him or bring joy to the people who loved to watch him perform. Later I wrote on Skidboot's website, "Skidboot is at rest. The bell of time has made its inevitable toll. What a wonderful life of fourteen years he lived. Never has a last-minute, second-thought Christmas gift ever shone so brightly as Skidboot." We asked people to remember Skidboot with donations in his name to their local animal shelters.[2]

Barbara and I buried Skidboot with his favorite toy beneath an oak tree on the property he had helped us purchase. Our other dogs and some friends joined us as we laid a memorial of two pieces of Austin limestone on his gravesite.

The first performance I did, a week after Skidboot's passing, was in Santa Barbara, California. It was a fundraiser for the Santa Barbara County Animal Care Foundation, and I was performing for a very sophisticated crowd of philanthropists. I said, "I guess y'all deserve to hear a little bit about Skidboot's life." I started telling them stories, and I broke up. When I couldn't talk anymore, I apologized. That's the worst it's been.

Every now and then, I think about him. I'll start telling somebody about him and get a frog in my throat. But usually I just remember lots of smiles and how much fun that dog had. Skidboot had no regrets.

Skidboot's Mission

Sometimes people have said that I found a wonderful ministry. I had no idea that talking and playing with my dog for an audience would become a ministry. I get comments like, "I bet you spent hours training Skidboot." I didn't. Skidboot learned everything so quickly and could do things I hadn't even taught him. So I say, "I didn't train this dog. God trained this dog. I'm just having fun."

Once, at Texas A&M College of Veterinary Medicine, where I was one of the speakers entertaining at an open house, a lady came up to Skidboot and me. She said, "I've been under treatment for breast cancer for the last several weeks, and I've been miserable. I've felt so wonderful just watching. You and that dog have allowed me to smile and feel good for the first time in weeks." Skidboot had made her feel better in the midst of a hard time.

We got a card from a woman who saw us on television. She said that she wanted to thank us for demonstrating patience, understanding, unconditional love, intelligence, and a whole list of virtues that she thought Skidboot had. We got so many cards and emails that said it really wasn't about the dog's tricks but the love people saw in the bond between Skidboot and me. I think, if you believe your teacher genuinely likes you, you'll give your all. If you love your teacher, you'll be eager to please.

In Coming Years

In New York there's a lady who talks telepathically to pets. I'm not a big believer in stuff like this, but Barbara called the lady after Skidboot died. The lady sent an email that said she had talked to Skidboot from the other side. According to her, Skidboot said that he wanted to communicate that he felt nothing but love from me. He appreciated all of the fans who supported him and felt nothing but love from them. The lady said Skidboot told her that he was most proud of the fact that he got a lot of different people in this world to think differently about animals. She added that his work was not nearly through and let us know that Skidboot's work has only just begun.

Maybe she was reflecting what Skidboot's purpose was, to make more people think of animals less judgmentally. They're not disposable, not "just animals." They're not meant to be tossed aside or neglected.

Skidboot created another career for me. He made me realize that my rodeoing needed to be on the back burner. This was a blessing in disguise, because I was trying to do something my old body wasn't capable of anymore.

What's a nearly fifty-year-old guy to do? First, one hip went out, then the other hip and a shoulder too. I never considered retirement. The dog stepped in and made me feel as if I had lots of things to do. He taught me that there was a big demand for homespun, wholesome entertainment, something new and different for kids, grandparents, and all ages to enjoy. I have plenty of options besides being a worn-out, old horseshoer and calf roper.

I believe that Skidboot was not my dog. I think he was God's dog, left in my custody. He was given to me. I always like to say that Skidboot was half blue heeler and half gift from God.

I give the credit and glory to God. Skidboot shows that there's a working God who is very involved with all of our lives. God does perform a number of miracles. Skidboot was sort of a little miracle to get people's attention.

MEDITATION

What are your most memorable moments when a dog or dogs made you laugh and helped you appreciate the gifts in your life?

Rescued by a Dog Named Leaf

Allen Anderson
Minneapolis, Minnesota

*F*our months after we lost our beloved yellow Labrador retriever, Taylor, to cancer in June 2006, we found a black cocker spaniel at the Animal Humane Society in Golden Valley, Minnesota. The card attached to his kennel at the animal shelter had only one word typed on it in the section labeled history: "Abandoned."

From the moment my wife, Linda, and I met this little guy, we couldn't get him out of our minds. We needed time to maturely reflect on such an important decision, so we asked the shelter to hold the dog for twenty-four hours. Then we drove home to have a "discussion" with the two cats and cockatiel, who would be affected by a new family member in our home.

They didn't say much about whether or not a dog would disrupt their lives. Later, they would express many strong opinions, mostly negative at first. Not having the heart to make the wiggly dog stay at the shelter one more night, we drove back to pick up the little fellow shortly before adoption hours ended.

At the checkout counter, where we submitted our paperwork requesting an adoption, a young attendant told us that this purebred cocker spaniel was physically in very good shape. He had been dumped at a different branch of this shelter outside the Twin Cities about a week earlier with another dog. The couple that left him hadn't provided any background since they had dropped him off after hours. They had left a note that said the dog's name was Harley. The shelter's veterinarian estimated Harley to be around a year old.

We brought Harley to our car and began to drive this nervous, uprooted little dog to the park before introducing him to his new home. When we stopped at a red light, a Harley-Davidson motorcycle roared up next to us. Harley's ears flailed back. He bared his teeth

Allen and Linda's Leaf

and glared at the biker, growling menacingly. Linda and I looked at each other and said, "This fellow does *not* want to be named Harley!"

So what name did he want to be called?

As soon as we started to walk with the dog around Lake Harriet at the park on this crisp autumn day, we discovered that he loved leaves. He chased, rolled, and played with abandon in piles of leaves. As he trotted along the pathway, he watched, fascinated, when auburn, yellow, and pumpkin-colored leaves tumbled from the trees.

We named him Leaf.

Almost immediately after taking Leaf home, we realized that his past experiences had scarred him and indicated that he'd been abused. He unexpectedly bolted away upon meeting certain types of people, such as heavyset, white males. One animal communicator thought that Leaf had been in a dreadful puppy mill. Many purebred dogs were sold from these awful places to pet stores, where people bought them without realizing that the pups had been treated inhumanely and might soon have behavior problems. Animal shelters are the sad recipients of many puppy mill–pet store dogs.

Another animal communicator said that, with great shame and embarrassment, Leaf had admitted his darkest secret to her with the words, "I got left."

It was obvious that Leaf wasn't accustomed to being inside a house, because he had no concept of indoors and outdoors. He certainly hadn't met any cats. He tried to play with and sniff them like dogs. At first, Leaf didn't seem to think that letting the cats have their space and quiet time was of high importance, but their claws and hisses taught him better.

The pain he felt from his abandonment ran deep. He constantly needed to be with either Linda or me. He would fall asleep and wake up disoriented with anxiety that escalated into full-blown panic attacks. His eyes would glaze over with fear, and he'd shriek with massive, wolflike howls. We spoke calm, reassuring words of love to him. Slowly he'd return to us from whatever terror and neglect he'd relived.

Leaf Begins to Heal

Over the winter months and into spring, Leaf became more secure in his new home, and the panic attacks lessened in frequency and severity. I identified with Leaf's insecurities. Growing up in a military family, I had moved from place to place a lot and knew what it felt like to have an uncertain future. Without judgment and with mutual empathy, Leaf and I accepted the baggage we each carried into our relationship. Also, I started to heal from the pain I'd felt over the loss of our beloved Taylor as Leaf and I became pals, buddies, and playmates.

When I took Leaf to a dog park near our home, I watched him play fearlessly with other dogs. Linda began calling him Alpha Dog of the World. No matter what size the dogs were, Leaf always seemed to position himself as leader of the pack. Despite whatever shattering experiences he'd had before coming to live with us, his confidence grew. His big ears flopped as he retrieved the balls I threw for him, and I felt great pleasure watching him become more carefree and curious. Life in our home seemed to be giving him the assurance he needed.

As the weeks passed, the love bond between Leaf and me strengthened. Initially, getting him accustomed to a new home with cats, a bird, and house rules was a lot of work. Middle-of-the-night bathroom walks outside in below-zero temperatures became commonplace.

In the past we had always had female dogs. Now we were living with this teenage "boy," who displayed a high degree of intelligence and had an agenda of his own. But through all the adjustments, he began to believe that we loved him. Unlike the frantic, terrified dog he had been only months earlier, by April 2007, he was showing his affection with kisses and play.

The Devastating Diagnosis

Leaf served as my stress reliever from the worries and pressure of my day job, which bristled with deadlines. The books that Linda and I authored required promotion, research, conducting interviews, and writing. So my evenings and weekends were filled with tasks.

When I had a couple of spells of vertigo, or dizziness, I did not think much of it, chalking it up to anxiety and too many to-do lists. During a regular exam I told my primary-care doctor about the dizziness. He ordered tests, including an MRI of the brain, to find out if there was a physical cause for the vertigo. I assumed it was due to an inner-ear infection, which is a common cause and easily treatable.

At last I had a pleasant weekend of nicely balanced work and dog-park play with Leaf. I had almost forgotten about my recent visit to the doctor. I loved watching Leaf run with certain dog friends. He played hard and enjoyed himself immensely. I had often written about his exploits in our weekly writer's group. I was having no more dizzy spells and believed all was right in my world.

After the restful weekend I went back in my office and was preparing for a conference call. My phone rang, but the caller was not whom I expected. I heard a man softly speak but, at first, did not catch what he had said. I asked, "Who is this again?"

"Allen, this is Doctor W.," the man on the other end of the line said. Then he told me that my X-rays showed what appeared to be an unruptured brain aneurysm. He said there was no cause for panic, but it was worthy of concern. I would need additional tests to determine the aneurysm's exact measurements. He explained that the aneurysm was located in the middle of my forehead about an inch deep, behind the skull. In a solemn, firm voice he said, "This needs attention."

After the phone call I walked into the hallway, feeling confused. The shock of what the doctor had told me and its possible consequences began to seep into my consciousness. What bizarre turn had my life taken?

I thought about the fact that my father had had a stroke when he was forty-nine years old. After that, I remembered him as a man filled with anger. His suffering and pain had endured for many years.

I don't know why, but at that moment, I saw Leaf's face in my mind's eye. I remembered his howling into the empty air whenever he felt abandoned. Then his anguished face disappeared from my inner vision. I suddenly felt alone and every bit as scared as my fearful, little dog.

Too Much Information

After doing some quick research, I learned that when these aneurysms rupture, most people don't survive. The typical scenario of someone whose aneurysm bursts is that the person says (or screams), "I'm having the worst headache of my entire life." Then the person dies immediately or soon after. Nothing I'd read so far relieved my anxiety in the least.

I left work early that day and decided to think about how to tell my wife about the brain aneurysm. I took Leaf to the dog park he loves so much. Usually he runs and joyfully plays. But that day, he wouldn't leave my side.

I looked down at Leaf, and he looked back at me with an expression that conveyed a deep, loving, and spiritual understanding. Somehow, he conveyed that he would be there for me. I was near tears at seeing this rambunctious "teenager" with so much pain in his past carrying yet another burden that should not be his. After all, he was still only a puppy.

All that afternoon at the dog park, Leaf stayed close to me instead of chasing the other dogs. Finally I found an old ball to throw so he could get some exercise while we were there.

By the next day, I had gathered more information about brain aneurysms. I even found some websites that proclaimed that when unruptured, like mine, aneurysms could be treated surgically. I finally talked with Linda about the diagnosis. Although I tried to remain calm for her sake, she had an emotional reaction, saying she loved me and didn't want to lose me. I understood. I feel the same way about her.

Soon after the phone call from my doctor, I went for a battery of tests. The highly skilled neurosurgeon to whom I had been referred needed detailed images and test results to make better recommendations on treatment. Unfortunately the tests found another life-threatening problem. Some blood clots, known as deep-vein thrombosis, in my upper leg could dislodge and launch on a direct path to my heart and brain, causing instant death.

Now I was dealing with not just one but two medical emergencies. With this new development there was only one treatment course available for the aneurysm, and that was invasive brain surgery to clip the aneurysm. This had to be done quickly so I could start taking blood-thinning medication to dissolve the clots.

My wife and I sat in the surgeon's office, numbly trying to take in all the medical terminology and facts. The research showed that, even with a successful brain surgery, side effects could include memory loss, headaches, loss of motor functions, and other horrors too numerous to list.

Preparing for the Worst

With Leaf lying at my feet one night and the surgery date fast approaching, I sat at my computer and began preparing to leave this world. I gathered important financial, insurance, medical, retirement, and legal information and other aspects of my complex life, and compiled a manual for Linda to use as reference if the worst happened. I arranged to update my will and made a living will. I felt overwhelmed at the thought of all the hospital procedures and medical tests. The future looked bleaker than I had ever imagined.

Leaf sprawled flat on the floor with all four legs splayed out, making him look like a piece of thick, black carpet. I smiled. He raised his head and focused on me with his dark, loving eyes. For an instant, I felt a glimmer of hope. With his help, this might turn out okay.

He plopped his head back down between his two front feet and let out a loud sigh. I realized that the ups and downs of my emotions must have been taking a toll on him as well. He looked exhausted.

I needed those moments that only Leaf could bring me. During the few weeks prior to my surgery, I had flashes of memories that reminded me of times and events I deeply regretted. I honestly wondered if my body and mind were letting me know that life as I had lived it was coming to an end. Was feeling regret over my missed opportunities a way of preparing for death?

The Worst Dream Ever

I didn't want to dwell on my fears, but anxiety surged as I worried that this surgery could go sour. I seemed to have no choice. I had to go through with it. With a bit of awe in their voices, the doctors had told me that I was incredibly fortunate to have had both of these conditions, a brain aneurysm and blood clots, found before they had done any damage. Mysteriously the dizziness that had prompted my primary-care doctor to order the MRI had completely disappeared. It has never returned and was not actually a symptom of either condition. Vertigo had merely triggered the whole process into motion.

I had a vivid dream that reinforced my concerns. It was so real that I'll never forget it. In the dream I stood outside a gigantic, domed structure. From that vantage point I watched thousands of people of all ages, races, and descriptions stand in a line that moved swiftly into the structure. The line seemed never ending. I knew some of the people very well. Others, I may have seen sometime in my life. But I did not remember ever meeting most of them.

I heard the people in line say that this was the Building of Life. They explained that it contained countless rooms filled with everything that could be imagined: art, all the books of the world, buildings of all kinds, forests, lakes, oceans, relationships, and families. All possible life experiences were represented in the massive structure. Everyone in line who had a ticket could experience room after room after entering the structure.

All of these people had a ticket — everyone except for me.

I looked for a ticket counter, but they were all closed. I panicked, thinking that this was a terrible mistake. I saw Linda, the love of my life, standing in line with our dear friends. They moved very fast, entering the structure and leaving me behind. Nobody looked back to acknowledge that I even existed.

Why did I not have a ticket? What had I done wrong? I was supposed to be with them. Why had I been left behind and abandoned? I tried to catch up, but Linda was so far ahead. How could I ever be with her again?

I was not allowed to continue. The dream indicated that I was dead to all those I had known and loved. I pushed my way into line, thinking no one would notice I did not have a ticket. Everyone noticed. All these people made sure I knew that I did not belong there. I was no longer one of them.

Devastated, I did not know what had happened. Linda was gone. This was it. I was alone and forgotten, as if I had never existed.

I woke up from the dream to Leaf's jumping on the bed, putting his paws on my shoulders, and licking my face. I gave him a big hug. While I do not know the details of his past, as I awakened from that nightmare, I understood a little more about the fear and pain he must have felt at having been abandoned.

That morning I told Linda about my dream. I noticed that Leaf listened intently to this conversation.

Through the next few days, prior to the surgery and after my devastating dream, Leaf developed what we thought was a behavior problem. He took newspapers, envelopes, and magazines off the living-room coffee table, threw them onto the floor, and shredded them into tiny pieces. After we discovered the mess he made, we asked, "Leaf, what are you doing?"

He picked up one of the smaller pieces of paper in his mouth and brought it to me. I started cleaning up the mess, and he brought me another sliver of paper — then another and another.

Surgery Day

"You have a few minutes. Do you want to go out and spend some time with your family?" the nurse asked. She had just placed white thrombosis stockings on my legs. This was the last of her duties in preparing me for brain surgery.

I said yes, forgetting how silly I looked in a gown, robe, white stockings, and the hospital's stylish, green socks. But I longed to see familiar faces, to talk with anyone who was important to me in this life.

I was glad that we had placed Leaf in his favorite doggy day care and boarding facility while I was in the hospital. Linda stayed at a nearby hotel. The staff at the day care center adored Leaf. Every time he arrived, they chanted, "Leaf, Leaf, Leaf." With the plasma-screen television always turned on to the Animal Planet channel, Leaf felt at home in this place.

Ever since I had checked into the hospital for surgery, I had seen Leaf in my inner vision. It seemed as if we had agreed to spiritually check in with each other, even though the miles separated us.

The nurse guided me through the hallway to the surgery waiting room, where I spotted Linda right away. It was a relief to see her. She looked happy that we could visit for a few minutes. My daughter Susan, sister Gale, and mother Bobbie had all flown in from Atlanta to see me through the surgery. Two dear friends, Arlene and Aubrey, also sat in the waiting room.

I walked over to this loving group, hugged everyone, and sat next to Linda. I glanced over at the fish tank. For an instant, in my mind's eye I saw a vision of Leaf's face gazing at me lovingly, and then it disappeared. In this brief vision I noticed that he was in the process of grabbing slips of paper off the living-room table and holding some of them in his mouth, just as he'd done at home recently. He looked happy, and I felt delighted to see him.

Concerned and apprehensive, I did not make light of my situation while family and friends surrounded me. Instead, I looked at each person and thanked him or her for all he or she had done to help. Throughout this ordeal I had felt the presence and protection of Divine Spirit, but as I sat there with my loved ones, I recalled the disturbing dream in which I'd watched myself being separated from them forever. I still didn't know what my fate would be. It all seemed so uncertain.

After I had hugged and said good-bye to everyone in the waiting room, the nurse escorted me back to the pre-op area. I lay down on the table, and the nurses placed warm blankets over me. The anesthetists, wearing blue scrubs, injected a tube in the vein in my arm. One of them explained that this would measure several things, including blood pressure and heartbeat rate.

Another man in a gray beard and glasses, who was also part of the surgical team, started an IV in the other arm and casually asked what I did. I said that my wife and I wrote books about the human-animal spiritual bond. Soon, the man told me about his dog and how special the animal had been to his family, especially his son.

My gurney was wheeled to the surgical suite. Strong arms lifted me from it onto the surgical table. I knew that soon I would no longer be conscious. I saw flashes of blue and white lights in the corner of the room, and felt a sense of being protected. In spite of all my previous fears, I remained surprisingly calm and wasn't scared anymore.

I watched as the anesthesiologist lowered the breathing mask until it hovered about ten inches above my face. As he slowly lowered it, I heard the bearded man on the surgical team say, "You are safe. We will be with you through it all."

Before the mask reached my mouth and nose, just as in the image I had seen in the waiting room, I again had a vision of Leaf's face. Although my perception may have been clouded from the presurgery IV that was supposed to relax me, what happened next was vivid and real, filled with mystical love from my canine friend. In that split second, my sweet cocker spaniel dropped the piece of paper he had gripped so tightly in his mouth, the one that resembled the slivers of paper he had tried to give me at home.

Unable to clearly see the tiny paper, I felt confused. In my inner vision, as if in a dream, I reached for the paper Leaf had dropped. I touched it and knew what it was. Tears filled my eyes. It was the ticket that had eluded me in my dream.

Leaf had brought me my ticket. Things would be okay. Along with family and friends, I would awaken from this surgery and enter the Building of Life. Calmly, I deeply inhaled the flow of air from the mask.

Fade to black.

My Leaf Recovery Program

After a successful surgery, I returned home from the hospital a week later. One afternoon during my recovery period, Leaf, Linda, and I sat on the couch together. Leaf gently rested his head on my lap. I sipped on a cup of tea.

I looked down at our little adopted dog and realized he was nothing less than a giant in my life. We had rescued him from an animal shelter where he had been left feeling alone and frightened. We had delivered him from what obviously was a painful and abusive situation. We had loved him and provided an enduring home that he had started to trust would not be taken away.

And yet, after all, by seeing me through the most difficult, challenging, and frightening experiences of my life, it was Leaf who had rescued me. He had been an angelic messenger, delivering a ticket from the Divine for access to all of life's promises.

Our dog named Leaf is my amazing hero and friend. He stayed at my side each step of the way as my healing and remaining recovery continued.

For now — dog park, play, and blessed normalcy.

MEDITATION

What miracles occurred in your life when a dog became your vehicle for a divine message?

Afterword

Coming to the end of a book about dogs and people who have given astonishing service feels like a bit of a letdown to us. The dogs in this book have reminded us that, in spite of all that is wrong with the world, many aspects of people and dogs are incredibly good and inspiring.

The list of services dogs provide to humans and other animals appears nearly endless. Dogs amaze us with their abilities, from using their superior senses of smell, hearing, and sight for the betterment of all to intuitively knowing and responding to suffering with sentient compassion. Not only are dogs highly capable of giving service to all life, they also seem to want to help out in any way they can. Sometimes it's for treats. Mostly, though, it's out of their honest, deep, and abiding love and loyalty.

Repeatedly, as we interviewed people for this book and gathered their stories, we marveled at the depth and breadth of human-dog relationships. It almost seemed that if anyone could identify a need, somehow a dog would find a way to fulfill it.

With two out of three American homes having pets, nearly seventy-five million of which are dogs, as a society we live in an unprecedented era.[1] For the first time in modern history, humans and canines by the millions share homes as family members. Close-up and personal, dogs are demonstrating their amazing minds, intuition, and capacity for unconditional love. People have the opportunity to observe dogs as examples of the spiritual rewards inherent in leading purposeful lives. While their dog companions thrive on discovering who they are meant to be and what they are born to do, people become inspired to lead more meaningful lives.

Why Dogs Are Angels

Angels are messengers from God. When people are in trouble or pain, angels appear to show that God has not abandoned them. We call dogs angels because they deliver the message that love truly is all around and blessings abound. We call dogs angels because they respond to human need and suffering with astounding specificity, providing exactly what people need when they need it. We call dogs angels because they protect others even as they risk their own lives. We call dogs angels because after they leave this world, their spiritual and loving presence and legacies live on.

Are all dogs angels? Dogs have the capacity for operating from the highest to lowest state of consciousness, just as humans do. But in terms of being pure vehicles for delivering messages, they can hardly be beat. In places where violence and evil prevail, dogs convey the consequences of inflicting pain on others. Where people move through life with grace and dignity, dogs guide their footsteps on paths of benevolence. Even when people follow their lowest impulses, dogs often rise above circumstances, training, and instincts to demonstrate a better way.

In this human-centric world, where people often forget that we're not the only ones occupying the planet and that humans are relative newcomers, dogs and other animals operate, for the most part, unnoticed and unappreciated as some of earth's wisest teachers. We hope the inspiring stories in this book have helped you catch glimpses of how profound canine awareness can be. It's only visible to those who look beyond preconceived notions. If you have to wait for whatever scientific research can tell you about canine capabilities, you'll be playing catch-up all the time.

Dogs express love with every wag of their tails and every beat of their golden hearts. They are souls that have accepted and embraced a mission of giving service to all life. Our lives are enriched when we have the humility, perception, and gratitude to accept the abundant blessings that angel-dog messengers bring into this world.

Acknowledgments

*W*e give our appreciation to Georgia Hughes, New World Library editorial director, who has worked with us on *Angel Dogs with a Mission* and made it her mission to bring the book's inspiring messages to the world.

We are grateful to the wonderful visionary Marc Allen, the marketing director and associate publisher Munro Magruder, our enthusiastic publicity manager Monique Muhlenkamp, managing editor Kristen Cashman, editorial assistant Jonathan Wichmann, type designer Tona Pearce Myers, art director Mary Ann Casler, copy editor Nelda Street, and all the staff at New World Library.

We sincerely appreciate the encouragement from Harold and Joan Klemp, which inspired us on our journey of giving service by writing books about the animal-human spiritual bond.

A special thanks to all the people who shared their stories about the many cherished experiences with dogs.

We appreciate the generosity and wisdom of those who served as judges for the contest we held to find stories for this book: Darlene Montgomery, Connie Bowen, Helen Weaver, The Reverend Mary Piper, Marcia Wilson, Von Braschler, and Jeff Dorson.

We extend our heartfelt gratitude to Stephanie Kip Rostan of Levine Greenberg Literary Agency, Inc., our dynamic literary agent, whose middle name is Encouragement.

Our families instilled a love of animals in us from an early age. We especially appreciate Allen's mother, Bobbie Anderson, and Linda's mother, Gertrude Jackson. To our son and daughter, Mun Anderson and Susan Anderson, you're the best. Much love to Allen's sister, Gale Fipps, and brother, Richard Anderson, and their families.

Special thanks to Darby Davis, editor of *Awareness* magazine, for publishing our column, "Pet Corner," all these years and to Kathy DeSantis and Sally Rosenthal for writing consistently beautiful book reviews. Lessandra MacHamer, you have always been in our corner, and we love you for it.

And thanks to our current animal editors: Leaf, Speedy, Cuddles, and Sunshine. Without you, we wouldn't have been able to fulfill our purpose.

Permissions Acknowledgments

P. 1 epigraph: From *Noble Purpose: The Joy of Living a Meaningful Life* by William Damon. Reprinted with permission of Templeton Foundation Press.

P. 91 epigraph: From *Man's Search for Meaning* by Viktor Frankl. Copyright © 1959, 1962, 1984, 1992 by Viktor E. Frankl. Reprinted by permission of Beacon Press, Boston.

P. 133 epigraph: From *Working Like a Dog* © 2003 by Gena K. Gorrell, published by Tundra Books of Northern New York.

P. 169 epigraph: From *How Dogs Think: Understanding the Canine Mind* by Stanley Coren. Copyright © 2004 by SC Psychological Enterprises Ltd. All rights reserved. Reprinted with the permission of the Free Press, a Division of Simon & Schuster Adult Publishing Group.

P. 205 epigraph: From Thomas Berry, "Prologue: Loneliness and Presence," in *A Communion of Subjects: Animals in Religion, Science, and Ethics,* edited by Paul Waldau and Kimberly Patton. Copyright © 2006 Columbia University Press. Reprinted with permission of the publisher.

Notes

Introduction: Service to All Life

Epigraph: Robert Frost, "Stopping by Woods on a Snowy Evening," *Complete Poems of Robert Frost* (New York: Holt, Rinehart, and Winston, 1964), 275.

Chapter One: A Mission to Serve

Epigraph: William Damon, *Noble Purpose: The Joy of Living a Meaningful Life* (Radnor, PA: Templeton Foundation Press, 2003), 91.

1. Friends of Utah Avalanche Center, "Avalanches: The Basics" and "Avalanche Accidents," www.avalanche.org/~uac/med-quick-facts.htm.
2. Canadian Avalanche Rescue Dog Association, "CARDA: Background and Training, and Certification Standards, January 2006," www.carda.bc.ca.
3. Ibid.
4. Fernie Alpine Resort, "The Avalanche Dog Rescue Program," www.skifernie .com/the-mountain/avalanche-rescue-dog-program.aspx.
5. Ted Bortolin and Todd Serotiuk, *Animal Miracles* (also known as *Miracle Pets*), episode 4, "Keno, Avalanche Dog," produced by Animal Miracles Production, Inc., 2001, www.imdb.com/title/tt0279543.
6. Purina Animal Hall of Fame, www.purina.ca/halloffame/default.asp?year=2002.
7. Bonnie Bergin, EdD, with Sharon Hogan, *Teach Your Dog to Read: A Unique Step-by-Step Program to Expand Your Dog's Mind and Strengthen the Bond between You* (New York: Broadway Books, 2006), 4.

Chapter Two: A Mission to Inspire

Epigraph: Judith Wright, *There Must Be More Than This: Finding More Life, Love, and Meaning by Overcoming Your Soft Addictions* (New York: Broadway Books, 2003), 37.

Chapter Three: A Mission to Heal

Epigraph: Viktor E. Frankl, *Man's Search for Meaning* (Boston: Beacon Press, 2006), 37.

1. Pine Street Foundation, "Research Update — Summer 2007," www.pinestreet foundation.org/articles/canine.html#top.

2. Ibid.

3. Michael McCulloch, Tadeusz Jezierski, Michael Broffman, Alan Hubbard, Kirk Turner, and Teresa Janecki, "Diagnostic Accuracy of Canine Scent Detection in Early- and Late-Stage Lung and Breast Cancers," *Integrative Cancer Therapies* 5 (2006): 1, 30–39 (accessed at Sage Journals Online, http://ict.sagepub.com /cgi/content/abstract/5/1/30).

Chapter Four: A Mission to Protect

Epigraph: Gena K. Gorrell, *Working Like a Dog: The Story of Working Dogs throughout History* (Plattsburgh, NY: Tundra Books of Northern New York, 2003), 145.

Chapter Five: A Mission to Teach

Epigraph: Stanley Coren, *How Dogs Think: Understanding the Canine Mind* (New York: Free Press, 2004), 290.

Chapter Six: A Mission to Bring Joy and Hope

Epigraph: Thomas Berry, "Prologue: Loneliness and Presence," ed. Paul Waldau and Kimberly Patton, *A Communion of Subjects: Animals in Religion, Science, and Ethics* (New York: Columbia University Press, 2006), 8.

1. Ron Westmoreland with David Hartwig, *Skidboot: The Amazing Dog* (Austin, TX: Eakin Press, 2002), 123.

2. David Hartwig, "David Hartwig, Skidboot, and Friends," www.skidboot.com.

Afterword

1. American Pet Products Manufacturers Association, Inc., 2007–2008 APPMA National Pet Owners Survey, quoted in Dick Donahue, "Reigning Cats and Dogs," *Publishers Weekly*, August 27, 2007, 32–39.

Contributors

Chapter One: A Mission to Serve

ROBIN SIGGERS, "Keno, the Wonder Dog, Delivers an Avalanche Miracle." Robin is the mountain operations manager at Fernie Alpine Resort in Fernie, British Columbia (www.skifernie.com), in the Lizard Range of the Canadian Rocky Mountains. He served as a senior ski patroller and handler in the Avalanche Rescue Dog Program with his dog Keno. He was trained through the Canadian Avalanche Rescue Dog Association (CARDA) and encourages people to donate money and woolen shirts and blankets to this wonderful organization that is dedicated to saving the lives of avalanche victims (www.carda.bc.ca).

BONITA M. BERGIN, PHD, "The Dogs Who Taught Me How Amazing Dogs Can Be." Bonita (Bonnie) invented the concept of the service dog in 1975 to assist people with disabilities. She is founder of Canine Companions for Independence (CCI), a nonprofit organization that was the first to train and place service dogs for people with mobility impairments. She later founded the Assistance Dog Institute, the only university offering master's and associate of science degrees in dog studies. She is author of *Bonnie Bergin's Guide to Bringing Out the Best in Your Dog* (New York: Little, Brown and Company, 1995) and *Teach Your Dog to Read* (New York: Broadway Books, 2006). Dr. Bergin has received numerous awards, including Oprah Winfrey's Use Your Life Award and the Council on Disability Rights Individual Achievement Award. Learn more at www.assistancedog.org.

KERRILL KNAUS-HARDY, "Abdul, the History-Making Service Dog." Kerrill has specialized in the study of animal behavior and practiced pet-assisted therapy for over thirty years. She worked with Bonnie Bergin at Canine Companions for Independence in California for fifteen years. She moved to a ten-acre ranch in Scotts Mills, Oregon, and created the Adaptive Riding Institute (www.adaptiveridinginstitute.org) to serve people with disabilities by providing riding lessons, custom horse training, adaptive equipment, and recreational horseback riding for people of all abilities. She also operates Companion Cavaliers (www.companioncavaliers.com). Even though Kerrill has lived her entire life with muscular dystrophy, with the help of her beloved animals and supportive family, she has enjoyed going to college; getting married to her husband, Del; raising her nephew, Shaan, from infancy; traveling to four countries; and sharing her ranch with dogs, cats, a peacock, a goat, and thirty horses.

Chapter Two: A Mission to Inspire

SHERIFF DAN MCCLELLAND, "The Littlest Police Dog in the World." Dan is the sheriff for Geauga County, Ohio. He lives with his wife and family dogs, Midge and Buffy. Dan can be reached at DMcClelland@co.geauga.oh.us.

E. J. FINOCCHIO, DVM, "Marvin Paints Pictures of Thankfulness." Dr. Finocchio is president of the Rhode Island Society for the Prevention of Cruelty to Animals. He brings Marvin, a disabled shelter dog he and his family adopted, to visit nursing homes, hospitals, schools, and other places where people need the message of hope for second chances that Marvin offers. To learn more, go to www.marvinfund.org and www.rispca.com.

LISA LAVERDIERE, "At-Risk Teens Train At-Risk Dogs." Lisa founded Home for Life sanctuary in 1997 as a new kind of long-term sheltering to provide loving, nurturing lifetime care for special-needs animals. She is the executive director of Home for Life and has an office in Stillwater,

Minnesota. The sanctuary is in Star Prairie, Wisconsin, on forty acres of undeveloped farmland. Home for Life's community-outreach programs allow their dogs and cats to participate in the Pet Peace Corps, which brings certified therapy dogs to nursing homes, hospitals, and women's domestic-violence shelters, and in the Peace Creatures® program in cooperation with the Tubman Family Alliance of the Twin Cities, among other programs. Learn more at www.homeforlife.org. The Renaissance Project holds its dog-training classes at Boys Totem Town (www.co.ramsey.mn.us/cc/boys_totem_town.htm).

SARAH R. ATLAS, "Whispering Secrets to Anna at Ground Zero." Sarah is a member of the New Jersey Task Force One Urban Search and Rescue Team. She shares her life and home with search-and-rescue partner Tango; her other canine partner, Kaylee, a human-remains recovery dog; and Szara, who is a pet-therapy dog. Sarah and her beloved dog, Anna, were featured in *Dog Heroes of September 11th: A Tribute to America's Search and Rescue Dogs*, by Nona Kilgore Bauer (Allenhurst, NJ: Kennel Club Books, 2006), and they have been guests on the TV show, *It's Your Call with Lynn Doyle*. Sarah is founder of the nonprofit 501c(3) charity, The Search & Rescue Dog Foundation, Inc. To learn more, visit www.sardogfoundation.org.

Chapter Three: A Mission to Heal

DI THOMPSON, "Angel Eyes." Di Thompson and her husband, Dan, have lived in Fredericksburg, Virginia, just south of Washington, D.C., for twenty-five years. For nearly twenty years, Di has been self-employed as a freelance graphic artist, and Dan is now a facilities manager for the Library of Congress at the National Audio-Visual Conservation Center in Culpeper, Virginia. Di sings in her church choir and a local community chorus, and is a soloist at weddings and other functions. She and Dan live with two papillons, Zip and Little Bit (the latter of whom was adopted through Papillon Club of America Rescue), and Annabel, a Manx cat adopted from their local SPCA. Di has had a lifelong love affair with pets and truly respects the miracles that animals can work in our lives.

GAIL C. PARKER, "Say a Little Prayer, Renegade." Gail was born loving animals and has always had them in her life. Her grandmother did make her give away a snake though. Gail eagerly learned to read and always loved books. When she discovered what being an author meant, she wanted to write too. She has realized her childhood dream of becoming an author by writing for dog magazines. She lives with her fourth Irish setter, named Katie, and four cats, all from rescue groups. Her husband, Carl, is very supportive of her efforts to help people and animals. Their home is in Philadelphia, Pennsylvania, in an old neighborhood where all the neighbors know each other.

KARLA ROSE, PHD, "Tuffy, My Canine Grief-Counseling Partner." Karla is a grief and traumatic-stress consultant from Boston, Massachusetts, who works with her canine partner, Tuffy, to assess and comfort first responders, victims, and witnesses on scene. They serve as the canine-clinician team for Critical Incident Stress Management (CISM) in Massachusetts. Karla and Tuffy are members of, and have trained extensively with, the International Critical Incident Stress Foundation (ICISF). Tuffy has received numerous accolades in only three years of service, including the 2007 Diamond Pet Foods Labor Dog Essay Contest. Tuffy was nominated for the Delta Society's Beyond Limits awards. He earned an honorary high-school diploma from the Lincoln Sudbury Regional High School for his service. Even as a puppy, Tuffy received media attention in the *Boston Globe* for his service to cancer patients. A newspaper in Germany reported on Karla and Tuffy's trauma work after the Virginia Tech disaster and other crises to which their team deployed. The pair extensively lectures and provides demonstrations on "Traumatic Stress Intervention" and the use of canines in prevention of post-traumatic stress disorder. Learn more about Dr. Rose and Tuffy at www.pawsitive-recovery.com.

MARIA FRIANEZA RIOS, "Kobi, the Cancer-Detection Dog." Maria has worked at Lucasfilm in San Francisco, California, for thirteen years and is the senior accounting manager for the licensing department. Her department licenses rights to toys and merchandise for the Star Wars and Indiana Jones movies. In her spare time Maria enjoys doing Philippine folk dancing and is a member of the LIKHA Pilipino Folk Ensemble. She has traveled around the world performing with the group. She and her husband, Richard Rios, have adopted Yogi, a Labrador mix, from an animal shelter. Yogi sometimes accompanies Richard to his job at a pet hotel in San Francisco. To learn more about Kobi's work as a cancer-sniffing dog and the Pine Street Foundation, visit www.pinestreetfoundation.org.

Chapter Four: A Mission to Protect

LT. COL. CHRISTOPHER P. COPPOLA, USAF, "The Dogs of War." Christopher is a lieutenant colonel in the U.S. Air Force and a pediatric surgeon. He has encountered brave and skillful military working-dog teams during his two deployments to Iraq in support of Operation Iraqi Freedom. His wife, Meredith Coppola, has compiled a book of his letters home, *Made a Difference for That One: A Surgeon's Letters Home from Iraq*. It is available from the publisher at www.iUniverse.com. Proceeds from the book benefit Fisher House, an organization that provides a home away from home for family members of injured veterans. Dr. Coppola publishes his writing regularly on his blog, www.MadeaDifference .blogspot.com. The Coppola family lives in Texas with their three sons, their standard poodle, Loki, and their sixteen-year-old cat, Cosmo.

REBECCA KRAGNES, "The Little Mother Who Saved My Life." Portions of this story were first published in *Petwarmers*, June 14, 2006, a publication of www.heartwarmers.com. Rebecca lives in Minneapolis with her husband and their Seeing Eye Dogs®. She is a pianist and composer who has recorded four CDs to date. Rebecca's third album, *Surrender*, was inspired by her three Seeing Eye Dogs®: Tanner, Shelly, and Wynell. Rebecca plays for her church and volunteers to speak on blindness and related topics for schools and organizations. She is an active member of the American Council of the Blind of Minnesota and Minnesota Guide Dog Users, Inc. Rebecca serves on the Qwest Consumer Advisory Panel and the Minnesota State Rehabilitation Council for the Blind. She volunteers as hotline coordinator for the golden-retriever rescue organization, Retrieve a Golden of Minnesota. Her website is www.rebeccak.com.

ANNA AND NEMAN BATES, "How Scooby-Doo Earned His Angel Wings." Anna and Neman have been married for seven years and have a three-year-old son, Zen. They have both always been animal lovers. Scooby-Doo was the first "child" raised by them together, and they believe he knows he's spoiled. Neman currently runs his own company that builds concrete swimming pools, and he's also following in his grandfather's footsteps by developing property. Anna is a registered nurse with a dermatology nursing certification and has worked in the dermatology field for the last six years. Zen, Scooby, and the cat, Raz, like to help their family with whatever is available to work on.

GLORIA BULLERWELL, "The Dog in Wolf's Clothing." Gloria is owner and manager of Buck-a-boo Acres, a guest ranch with a peaceful environment that welcomes ecotourists and people who want a unique experience with nature. Visit www.buck-a-boo-acres.com for more information.

Chapter Five: A Mission to Teach

DEB RICHESON, "I'm a Zoom Kid." Deb worked for a Fortune 500 company as a compensation analyst in the human resources department. She was born in Hiroshima, Japan, to Ed and Kay Chizue Mitchell, the best parents ever, and had four of the best brothers any sister could hope for. Deb is grandmother and legally adoptive mother to Caley, the most wonderful young man in the world. She feels much blessed to be married for twenty-three years to Dave, a wonderful, supportive husband who calmly and patiently listens to her many ideas. In her little spare time, Deb works with stained glass, creates and sews for family and friends, and curls up with minty hot chocolate and rereads *The Count of Monte Cristo* or *Jane Eyre* (her all-time favorite books). She is passionate about her entire family and about children and their education.

HEATHER MITTY, "My Dog-Training Partner Is a Dog." Heather is area pet-training instructor for PetSmart in Minnesota. She and her husband, Mike, live with three dogs, Lola, Carmen, and Bindhi, and two cats, Chairman Meow and Chanel. Bindhi hopes to be just like her big sister, Lola, when she grows up.

MRS. MINAL VISHAL KAVISHWAR, "Kutty and Goldie, India's First Animal-Assisted-Therapy Dogs." Mrs. Kavishwar is a clinical psychologist, and founder and president of the Animal Angels Foundation, based in Pune, Maharashtra, India (www.animalangels.org.in). She conducts research and speaks at conferences and to the media about animal-assisted therapy. She presented a paper on the same topic at the International Conference on Psychology at the National Institute of Mental Health and Neuroscience in Bangalore. She invites other psychologists and animal lovers to help her introduce the practice of animal-assisted therapy to India. Her foundation trains and provides animals for children and adults who are disabled or autistic and who have severe behavioral issues or physical impairments. She has also conducted animal-therapy projects for AIDS and cancer patients in India. Her animal therapists include mostly dogs but also a sprinkling of cats, rabbits, and fish.

Chapter Six: A Mission to Bring Joy and Hope

DAVID HARTWIG, "Skidboot's Journey." David is a horseshoer, cowboy, and entertainer from Quinlan, Texas. He is training more dogs in the tradition of the amazing Skidboot and performs with his dogs to raise funds for animal shelters. David is writing a screenplay about Skidboot and welcomes help in bringing the dog's life story to movie screens. To view Skidboot's performances or order DVDs and books, visit David's website at www.skidboot.com or email him at friends@skidboot.com.

ALLEN ANDERSON, "Rescued by a Dog Named Leaf." See video clips of Leaf in action at www.angelanimals.net.

About Allen and Linda Anderson

*A*llen and Linda Anderson are speakers, pet-expert consultants, and authors of a series of ten books about the spiritual relationships between people and animals. Their mission is to help people discover and benefit from the miraculous powers of animals. In 1996 they cofounded the Angel Animals Network.

In 2004 Allen and Linda Anderson were recipients of a Certificate of Commendation from Governor Tim Pawlenty in recognition of their contributions as authors in the state of Minnesota.

In 2007 their book *Rescued: Saving Animals from Disaster* won the American Society of Journalists and Authors Outstanding Book award.

Allen Anderson is a writer and photographer. He was profiled in Jackie Waldman's book, *The Courage to Give*. Linda Anderson is an award-winning playwright as well as a screenwriter and fiction writer. She is the author of *Thirty-Five Golden Keys to Who You Are & Why You're Here*. Allen and Linda teach writing at the Loft Literary Center in Minneapolis, where Linda was awarded the Anderson Residency for Outstanding Loft Teachers.

The Andersons share their home with a dog, two cats, and a cockatiel. They donate a portion of revenue from their projects to animal shelters and animal-welfare organizations.

Please visit Allen and Linda's website at www.angelanimals.net and send them stories and letters about your experiences with animals. At the website or by email, you may also request a subscription to the free email newsletter *Angel Animals Story of the Week*, which features an inspiring story each week.

Contact Allen and Linda Anderson at:
Angel Animals Network
PO Box 26354
Minneapolis, MN 55426
Website: www.angelanimals.net
Email: angelanimals@angelanimals.net

NEW WORLD LIBRARY is dedicated to publishing books and other media that inspire and challenge us to improve the quality of our lives and the world.

We are a socially and environmentally aware company, and we strive to embody the ideals presented in our publications. We recognize that we have an ethical responsibility to our customers, our staff members, and our planet.

We serve our customers by creating the finest publications possible on personal growth, creativity, spirituality, wellness, and other areas of emerging importance. We serve New World Library employees with generous benefits, significant profit sharing, and constant encouragement to pursue their most expansive dreams.

As a member of the Green Press Initiative, we print an increasing number of books with soy-based ink on 100 percent postconsumer-waste recycled paper. Also, we power our offices with solar energy and contribute to nonprofit organizations working to make the world a better place for us all.

Our products are available
in bookstores everywhere.
For our catalog, please contact:

New World Library
14 Pamaron Way
Novato, California 94949

Phone: 415-884-2100 or 800-972-6657
Catalog requests: Ext. 50
Orders: Ext. 52
Fax: 415-884-2199
Email: escort@newworldlibrary.com

To subscribe to our electronic newsletter, visit
www.newworldlibrary.com